THE BACKPACKERS

THE BACKPACKERS GUIDE TO HAWAI'I

Stuart M. Ball, Jr.

A KOLOWALU BOOK
UNIVERSITY OF HAWAI'I PRESS
HONOLULU

01 00 99 98 97 96   5 4 3 2 1

Library of Congress Cataloging-in-Publication Data

Ball, Stuart M., 1948–
    The backpackers guide to Hawai'i / Stuart M. Ball, Jr.
        p.   cm.
    "A Kolowalu Book."
    Includes bibliographical references and index.
    ISBN 0–8248–1785–0 (alk. paper)
        1. Backpacking—Hawaii—Guidebooks.   2. Hawaii—Guidebooks.
    I. Title.
    GV199.6B35   1996   96–41359
    796.5'1'09969—dc20   CIP

Maps by Manoa Mapworks, Inc.

Designed by Paula Newcomb

CONTENTS

Color photos follow pages 58 and 106

ACKNOWLEDGMENTS

Listed here are the good friends who joined me on one or more of the trips for this book. I thank them all for their support and company: Fred Dodge, Herman and Myra Dombrowski, John Fiel, John Hall, John Hoover and Marcia Stone, Carole K. Moon, Janice Nako, Grant Oka, Kost A. Pankiwskyj, Jason and Cera Sunada, Ken Suzuki, Joyce Tomlinson, and Deborah Uchida.

INTRODUCTION

Hawai'i is truly a paradise for backpackers. While tourists and locals alike flock to the beaches, the mountains and remote shorelines remain surprisingly deserted. This book aims to change that just a little. It will take you where few people go, to active volcanoes, lush valleys, cascading waterfalls, secluded beaches, and windswept ridges and sea cliffs.

This guidebook includes 13 of the best backpacking trips in the Islands. Ten of them are open to the public and are described in detail. The remaining three are closed trips and thus rate only a brief description in the Appendix.

Each trip has a section on highlights, directions to the trailhead, and a detailed description of the route day by day. Each day has a narrative covering points of interest, major hazards, and campsites along the trail. As applicable, there are short notes about the plants, birds, geology, history, and legends of the area. Each trip also has its own topographic map keyed to the route description.

As you will see, this guidebook is very detailed. The information in it, however, is neither perfect nor up-to-date because of changing conditions. A government agency revises its camping permit policy. New lava forces a trail to be rerouted. A winter storm causes a landslide that blocks the route. Do not rely entirely on this book; use your own judgment and common sense, as well.

Good luck and good backpacking!

BACKPACKING TIPS

Climate

Hawai'i has two seasons, summer (May to October) and winter (November to April). Summer is the warmer and drier season. Daytime temperatures at sea level are in the eighties, and nighttime temperatures, in the seventies. Trade winds from the northeast blow steadily to cool the islands. The trades, however, do produce cloud buildup over the mountains and some rain.

Winter is the cooler and wetter season. Daytime temperatures at sea level are in the 70s and low 80s, and nighttime temperatures, in the 60s and low 70s. The winds are variable in strength and direction, sometimes coming from the south or west. Southerly Kona winds produce mainland type weather—clear skies or heavy cloud cover and rain.

Clothing

Listed below is the basic clothing you need to take on a backpacking trip in Hawai'i. The high altitude trips require additional clothing that is described in their Planning sections.

    sturdy hiking boots, leather or leather/fabric
    rubber slippers
    heavy outer socks
    light inner socks
    shorts, cotton or cotton blend
    lightweight pants, cotton or cotton blend (no jeans)
    lightweight shirt, short or long sleeved, cotton or cotton blend
    underwear top, synthetic fabric
    jacket or sweater, wool or synthetic fabric
    breathable rain jacket
    broad brimmed hat

Equipment

Listed below is the basic equipment you need to take on a backpacking trip in Hawai'i. Some of the trips require special equipment that is described in their Planning sections.

    backpack, internal or external frame
    light daypack

tent (leakproof!)
ground cover
mattress pad
light sleeping bag or liner
water bottle
water purifier or filter
first aid kit
flashlight with extra bulb and batteries
knife
compass
topographic maps
sunglasses
sunscreen
toilet paper
food
fuel
cooking gear
other personal gear

Pack It Out

Most of the trips in this book are trash free. Let's keep them that way. Pack out all your trash, including cigarette butts, gum wrappers, orange peels, and apple cores.

Clidemia hirta

Clidemia is an aggressive weed that overgrows some of the trails in the wet sections of the Big Island and Oʻahu. The shrub is easily recognized by its bright green elliptical leaves, which are heavily creased. Mature plants have hairy blue berries containing lots of tiny seeds.

Clidemia is spread by birds, and, yes, hikers. Clean the soles and sides of your boots carefully after doing the Waimanu Valley or Koʻolau Summit trips.

Emergencies

Don't have any! Seriously, come prepared with the right clothing and equipment. Constantly be aware of the route you are traveling and its possible hazards. Use your common sense and good judgment at all times.

All of the trips in this book travel to remote areas. If you get into trouble, do not expect to be rescued immediately. You are on your own.

Always tell someone where you are backpacking and when you will be out. Make sure they know to call the emergency number (911) and ask for Fire Rescue if you don't call or show up on time.

Hazards

There are hazards in backpacking, as in any sport. Described below are the main hazards you should be aware of while backpacking in Hawai'i. With the right equipment and good judgment on your part, you should be able to avoid or minimize these hazards and have an enjoyable trip.

Too Hot:

Backpacking in Hawai'i is usually a hot, sweaty experience. Drink plenty of water throughout the trip as it is very easy to become dehydrated. Prolonged lack of water can lead to heat exhaustion and heat stroke.

The sun in Hawai'i is very strong, even in winter. During midday wear a broad brimmed hat and use lots of sunscreen. Be particularly careful of the sun on the high altitude trips, Mauna Loa and Haleakalā.

Too Cold:

Backpacking in Hawai'i can also be a wet, cold experience. Insufficient or inappropriate clothing leads to chilling, which leads to hypothermia. Be prepared for rain on all the trips. On Mauna Loa and Haleakalā be prepared for nighttime temperatures at or below freezing.

Use the general clothing and equipment lists in this book as a guideline. Some of the trips have specific requirements which are described in their Planning sections.

Altitude Sickness:

Altitude sickness occurs when you climb to a high elevation too quickly for your body to adjust to the thin air. Symptoms can show up as low as 8,000 feet, depending on the individual. Symptoms include shortness of breath, headache, dizziness, loss of appetite, nausea, and general fatigue. The cure is to stop climbing, rest, drink plenty of liquids, and eat sparingly. If the symptoms persist or get worse, descend to a lower elevation immediately.

Mauna Loa and, perhaps, Haleakalā are the only trips where you may experience altitude sickness. Before attempting either one, read its detailed trip narrative thoroughly.

Leptospirosis:

Leptospirosis is a bacterial disease found in freshwater ponds and streams contaminated with the urine of rats, mice, and mongooses. The bacteria can enter the body through the nose, mouth, eyes, or open cuts.

Symptoms resemble those of the flu—fever, chills, sweating, head and muscle aches, weakness, diarrhea, and vomiting. They may persist for a few days to several weeks. In rare cases the symptoms may become more severe and even lead to death.

What to do? First, never drink any stream water unless you have adequately boiled, filtered, or chemically treated it. That's easy. Second, wear long pants to avoid getting cut and don't go swimming in freshwater. That's harder to do. After all, people come to Hawai'i to wear shorts and go swimming. Only you can decide how much risk you are willing to take.

Trips where leptospirosis may lurk are the ones with freshwater streams—Waimanu Valley, Kalalau, Mōhihi-Koai'e, Ko'olau Summit, and Mākua Rim.

High Streams:

Island streams can rise suddenly during heavy rainstorms. Do not cross a fast flowing stream if the water is much above your knees. Wait for the stream to go down. It is far better to be stranded for half a day than swept away.

The trips crossing major streams are Waimanu Valley, Kalalau, and Mōhihi-Koai'e.

Narrow Trail:

Hawai'i is known for its knife-edge ridges and sheer cliffs. Trails in those areas tend to be very narrow with steep drop-offs on one or both sides. Oftentimes, the footing is over loose rock or slick mud.

If narrow sections make you feel overly uneasy, don't try them. There is no shame in turning back if you don't like what you see. All the trips in this book have some narrow spots, except for Mauna Loa and Nāpau Crater.

Rough Lava:

Lava is tough on your boots and feet. Wear sturdy hiking boots with plenty of ankle support and cushioning. Don't take new boots on lava unless you want to age them prematurely!

As you will soon find out, there are two types of lava, 'a'ā and pāhoehoe. 'A'ā flows are jumbled up heaps of rough clinkery lava. They are virtually impassable without a trail. Even a well-worn path through ʻaʻā is difficult to walk on because of all the loose, uneven rock.

Pāhoehoe is lava with a smooth or, sometimes, ropy surface. The terrain of a pāhoehoe flow ranges from relatively flat to very humpy. A well-used trail on older pāhoehoe makes for easy hiking. Be careful, though, on new flows without an established treadway. Their crust may be thin and brittle in spots and can collapse when walked on.

The trips over lava are Halapē, Kaʻaha, Mauna Loa, Nāpau Crater, and Haleakalā.

Goat/Pig/Bird Hunters:

On the trips in the state forest reserves you may meet goat, pig, or bird hunters. They are friendly people, and their dogs generally are too. They use hiking routes to access hunting areas; however, the hunt usually takes place off trail.

Stay away from areas where you hear shots being fired or dogs barking. Trips where you may see or hear hunters are Waimanu Valley, Kalalau, Mōhihi-Koaiʻe, Koʻolau Summit, and Mākua Rim.

Marijuana (pakalōlō) Growers:

The danger from marijuana growers and their booby traps is much exaggerated. The growers do not plant their plots near recognized trails. All of the trips in this book travel on established routes. Stay on the trail, and you should have no pakalōlō problems.

The Ocean:

All of the shoreline trips visit remote beaches with no lifeguards. If you decide to swim, you're on your own. Ocean swimming is usually less hazardous in summer and along the leeward coasts, such as on the Halapē and Kaʻaha trips. The waters off Waimanu and Kalalau are particularly treacherous because of large swells and strong currents.

While exploring along the coast, remember the saying—never turn your back on the ocean.

Tsunami:

Tsunami are huge sea waves that can rapidly inundate coastal areas. The waves are generated by earthquakes, either locally or along the Pacific Rim.

If you feel an earthquake or you see the ocean recede suddenly, move to high ground immediately. The trips susceptible to tsunami are the shoreline ones—Halapē, Kaʻaha, Waimanu Valley, and Kalalau.

Hurricanes:

Hurricane season in Hawai'i is usually from June to December. Before starting a trip during that period, check the weather report to make sure no hurricanes are in the vicinity of the Islands.

A Final Caution

The hazards just described are the main ones you may encounter, but the list is by no means all inclusive. Like life in general, backpacking in Hawai'i carries certain risks, and no trip is ever completely safe. **YOU HAVE TO DECIDE HOW MUCH RISK YOU ARE WILLING TO TAKE.**

TRIP CATEGORIES

Type

There are two basic types of trips: shoreline and mountain. Obviously, shoreline trips are along the coast, and mountain trips, in the interior.

Length

Length gives the time in days and the distance in miles. For most trips, time is shown as a range of days. The lower value indicates the minimum time to complete the basic route. The upper value includes extra time for daytrips, layover days, and a more leisurely hiking pace.

Distance given is for the basic route to the nearest tenth of a mile. The mileage is taken from park signs or trail maps, when available. Otherwise, distance is measured on the U.S. Geological Survey topographical maps. The plotted value is then increased by 10 to 20 percent to account for trail meandering too small to be shown on the map.

Elevation Gain/Loss

Elevation gain and loss includes only significant changes in altitude. No attempt is made to account for all the small ups and downs along the route.

Measurements are taken from the U.S. Geological Survey topographic maps and then rounded to the nearest 100 ft. The gain and loss for the entire trip includes only the elevation changes along the basic route, not the suggested day hikes.

Difficulty

Difficulty attempts to roughly rank the trips in terms of the energy expended and hazards faced. The categories are low, medium, and high. Trips of low difficulty generally follow a well-graded and marked trail with gradual elevation changes and few hazards. High difficulty trips have a rough, sometimes obscure route with significant elevation changes and multiple hazards. Trips of medium difficulty fall somewhere in between.

How difficult a trip seems to you depends on your backpacking experience and physical fitness. An experienced conditioned backpacker will find the low difficulty trips easy, and the high difficulty trips, hard. An out-of-shape beginner may well find even the low difficulty trips challenging.

Use the difficulty rating only as a rough guide. Read the route description and the day narratives to get a better feel for the trip.

Location

Location tells the general area of the trip. Given is the island, and the mountain range, if applicable. Also mentioned is the national park, state park and/or state forest reserve where the trip is to be found.

Topo Map

Topo map refers to the U.S. Geological Survey quadrangle that shows the area of the trip. All maps referenced are in the 7.5 minute topographic series with a scale of 1:24,000 and a contour interval of 40 ft.

You can purchase topographic maps directly from the Geological Survey. Their address is USGS Map Sales, P.O. Box 25286, Federal Center, Building 810, Denver, CO 80225.

In Honolulu, topo maps for all the islands are available from Pacific Map Center at 560 N. Nimitz Hwy; phone (808) 545–3600 and Hawaii Geographic Maps & Books at 49 S. Hotel St. Suite 218; phone (808) 538–3952.

Highlights

Highlights briefly describes the trip and its major attractions.

Planning

This section provides information you need to know before actually starting the trip. Given are sources for park/reserve brochures, camping permits, and trail maps. Also included are the best time of year to take the trip and any special clothing or equipment requirements. Finally, this section mentions nearby airports, stores to buy food and fuel, and facilities at the trailhead.

Trailhead Directions

Trailhead directions are detailed driving instructions to the start of the trip. On O'ahu the directions start from downtown Honolulu. On the other islands, locally known as the Neighbor Islands, directions begin at the major airport nearest the trailhead.

If you are at all familiar with the islands, these directions should be sufficient to get you to the trailhead. If this is your first visit, bring along James A. Bier's reference maps to supplement the directions. His maps for each island can be purchased locally at bookstores and tourist shops.

All the drives to the beginning of the trips are all over paved roads, suitable for rental cars. At the trailhead never leave valuables in your vehicle.

Day Narrative

Each day of the trip has a narrative section, as well as a route description. At the beginning is the length in miles and elevation gain and loss in feet for the day. Following is a brief narrative of the day's route, its difficulty, major hazards, and points of interest. As applicable, there are short notes about the plants, birds, geology, history, and legends of the area. At the end is a description of the campsite and its facilities. On layover days this section suggests short hikes or other activities.

Route Description

This section provides a detailed description of the route for each day of the trip. Noted are junctions, landmarks, and points of interest. Also described are specific hazards, such as a rough, narrow trail section.

Each trip has its own map. The solid line shows the route. The letters indicate important junctions or landmarks and are keyed to the route description. For example, map point A is always the trailhead where you start the trip.

The maps are reproductions of the U.S. Geological Survey quadrangles for the immediate area of the trip. As in the originals, the scale is 1:50,000, and the contour interval is 20 meters. That roughly converts to 65 feet as one meter equals 3.281 feet.

The maps in this book should only be used for planning because of their small scale and summarized features. On the actual trip use the U.S. Geological Survey quadrangles with a scale of 1:24,000 and a contour interval of 40 feet. The quadrangles you need are listed under each trip.

This section sometimes uses Hawaiian words to describe the route. They are listed below with their English definition.

'a'ā—rough, clinkery lava
ahu—a pile of rocks indicating the route through treeless areas; known as cairns on the mainland
kīpuka—an island of vegetated older lava surrounded by newer flows
makai—seaward; toward the ocean
mauka—inland; toward the mountains
pāhoehoe—smooth, sometimes ropy lava
pali—cliff
pu'u—peak or hill

The word *contour* is sometimes used in the route description as a verb, that is, to contour. It means to hike roughly at the same elevation across a slope. Contouring generally occurs on trails that are cut into the flank of a ridge and work into and out of each side gulch.

Options

Options points out any alternatives to the basic route and describes the possible variations in time spent on the trip. The section also briefly mentions any optional day hikes.

Trip Summary (Part 1)

TRIP	ISLAND	TYPE	DAYS	LENGTH(MI)	ELEV. GAIN/LOSS (FT)	DIFFICULTY
1. Halapē	Hawaiʻi	Shoreline	2–3	19.3	100/2,300	Medium
2. Kaʻaha	Hawaiʻi	Shoreline	3	14.6	2,300/2,300	Medium
3. Mauna Loa	Hawaiʻi	Mountain	3–6	38.2	6,600/6,600	High
4. Nāpau Crater	Hawaiʻi	Mountain	2–3	12.2	0/1,200	Low
5. Waimanu Valley	Hawaiʻi	Shoreline	2–3	18.0	3,600/3,600	Medium
6. Kalalau	Kauaʻi	Shoreline	2–4	22.0	2,400/2,400	Medium
7. Mōhihi-Koaiʻe	Kauaʻi	Mountain	2–3	19.6	1,400/1,400	Low
8. Haleakalā	Maui	Mountain	2–4	20.0	2,400/4,200	Medium
9. Koʻolau Summit	Oʻahu	Mountain	3	19.5	2,900/1,700	High
10. Mākua Rim	Oʻahu	Mountain	2–3	13.5	1,100/1,100	Low

Trip Summary (Part 2)

TRIP	MAJOR ATTRACTIONS	MAJOR HAZARDS
1. Halapē	stark, windswept coast sandy beach fringed with palm trees swimming, snorkeling, historical sites	rough lava hot sun
2. Kaʻaha	stark, windswept coast sea arches and black sand beach swimming, snorkeling, lava tubes	rough lava hot sun
3. Mauna Loa	massive, still active volcano pit craters, spatter cones, steam vents, lava flows, star gazing	high altitude rough lava cold weather
4. Nāpau Crater	active volcano and native rain forest pit craters, spatter cones, steam vents, lava flows, tree molds	rough lava
5. Waimanu Valley	lush, wide valleys and narrow gulches black sand beaches and vertical sea cliffs waterfalls, swimming, historical sites	high streams narrow spots powerful surf
6. Kalalau	valleys and gulches with towering ridges wide, sandy beaches and sheer sea cliffs waterfalls, swimming, historical sites	high streams narrow spots powerful surf
7. Mōhihi-Koaiʻe	deep canyons native rain forest and swamp native birds	high streams
8. Haleakalā	dormant volcano with huge crater spatter cones, lava tubes native plants and birds, star gazing	high altitude cold weather
9. Koʻolau Summit	lush, wide valleys and narrow gulches summit lookouts and vertical cliffs native plants and birds	overgrown, obscure route narrow spots
10. Mākua Rim	dry leeward valleys and gulches summit lookouts and vertical cliffs native dry-land forest	narrow spots

HAWAI‘I

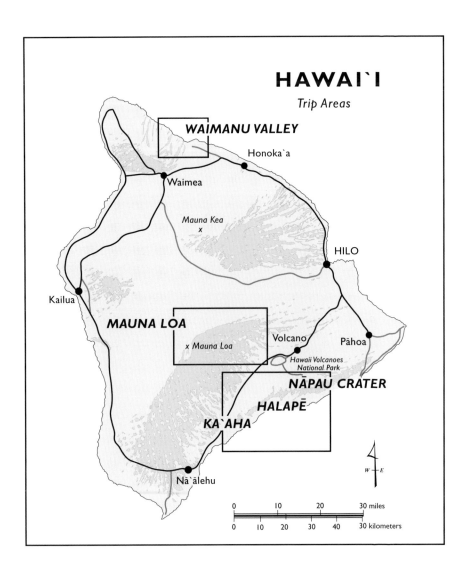

HAWAI`I

Trip Areas

WAIMANU VALLEY

Honoka`a

Waimea

Mauna Kea
x

HILO

Kailua

MAUNA LOA

x *Mauna Loa*

Volcano

Pāhoa

*Hawaii Volcanoes
National Park*

NĀPAU CRATER

HALAPĒ

KA`AHA

Nā`ālehu

W — E

| 0 | | 10 | | 20 | | 30 miles |

| 0 | 10 | 20 | 30 | 40 | 30 kilometers |

1 Halapē

Type:	Shoreline
Length:	2–3 days, 19.3 mi
Elev. Gain/Loss:	100/2,300 ft
Difficulty:	Medium
Location:	Hawai'i (the Big Island): Hawai'i Volcanoes National Park
Topo Map:	Ka'ū Desert, Makaopuhi Crater

Highlights

With its white sand beach and shady palm trees, Halapē is an idyllic oasis along the barren, windswept Ka'ū coast. The route descends a 1,500-foot cliff, known as Hilina Pali, and passes a series of faults with cracks and lava tubes. The way out, along the coast, is all sun, sand, sea, wind, and lava.

Planning

Call or write the National Park for a brochure, trail map, and camping information. The visitor center phone number is (808) 967–7311, and the address is Superintendent, Hawai'i Volcanoes National Park, HI 96718.

Winter (November–April) is the best time of year to take this trip. The temperature then is cooler, and the sun less intense. If you must do the trip in summer, use plenty of sunscreen and drink lots of water. The only shade along the coast is in the shelters or underneath the palm trees.

Bring a tent as Halapē Shelter is overrun with cockroaches and mice at night. Take a light sleeping bag or liner as nights can be chilly, especially in winter. *Tabis* (Japanese reef walkers) with their fuzzy soles are perfect for exploring the slippery, rocky shoreline.

If possible, plan to arrive on the Big Island at Hilo. The driving instructions below start from the Hilo Airport. All major rental car firms have booths there.

There is a public bus, known as Hele-on, from Hilo to the National Park once a day. Call the Hawai'i County Transit System at (808) 935–8241 for the current schedule.

If you are arriving at Keāhole Airport near Kailua (Kona), you have a longer drive. Exit Keāhole Airport and turn right on Queen Ka'ahumanu Hwy (Rte 19) to Kailua (Kona). There, pick up Hawai'i Belt Rd. (Rte 11)

3

and follow it around the southern tip of the island to the National Park. The distance to the trailhead is 118 miles and the driving time, about 3¼ hours.

Coleman fuel (white gas) is available at the 7-Eleven stores in Hilo, Hirano Store in Glenwood, and Volcano Store in Volcano. All three have some food items. For a wider selection stop at Safeway in the Prince Kūhiō Plaza or KTA Super Stores. Both are along Kanoelehua Ave. on the way out of Hilo.

Once in the park stop at the Kīlauea Visitor Center to get a backcountry permit. The center is open from 7:30 A.M. to 4:45 P.M. seven days a week. Check on the water supply at Halapē Shelter. Fill your water bottles for the first day as there is no water available at the trailhead.

Trailhead Directions

Distance: (Hilo Airport to Hilina Pali trailhead)—46 mi

Driving Time: 1½ hr

Exit Hilo Airport on Airport Rd.

At the first traffic light, turn left on Kanoelehua Ave. (Rte 11) to Volcano.

Kanoelehua Ave. becomes Hawai'i Belt Rd. (still Rte 11).

Just past Kea'au, the road narrows to two lanes.

Ascend gradually, passing the villages of Kurtistown, Mountain View, and Glenwood.

Pass turnoffs to Volcano village on the right.

Enter Hawai'i Volcanoes National Park.

Shortly afterward, turn left at the sign for the park entrance.

Pay the fee at the entrance station.

Stop at Kīlauea Visitor Center on the right (elev. 3,974 ft). There, get a backcountry permit for Halapē and ask about current trail conditions. Remember to fill your water bottles.

Drive back toward the entrance station.

Just before reaching it, turn right on Crater Rim Dr.

Turn left at the stop sign.

Pass Kīlauea Iki overlook on the right and Thurston (Nāhuku) lava tube on the left.

Wind through a tree fern and 'ōhi'a forest.

Pass the turnoff to Pu'u Pua'i on the right.

At the next intersection turn left on Chain of Craters Rd.

Pass turnoffs to Puhimau Crater on the left and Kokoʻolau Crater on the right.

Turn right on Hilina Pali Rd.

Pass Kīpuka Nēnē campground on the left.

Reach the end of the road at Hilina Pali overlook (elev. 2,280 ft) (map point A). If you have only one car, park it in the lot next to the picnic shelter and start hiking. If you have two cars, drop off people and packs, as necessary, and drive back on Hilina Pali Rd. in both cars.

Turn right on Chain of Craters Rd.

Pass the turnoff to Mauna Ulu on the left.

Pass turnouts marked Mau Loa o Mauna Ulu and Kealakomo on the right.

Descend Hōlei Pali on two switchbacks.

Look for a turnout marked Puʻuloa petroglyphs (elev. 140 ft) (map point R). Park one car there.

In the other car backtrack to the Hilina Pali overlook. The drive from the overlook to Puʻuloa and back again is 46 miles and takes about 1 ¼ hours.

DAY ONE—Hilina Pali overlook to Halapē

Length: 8.0 mi

Elev. Loss: 2,300 ft

Before starting, spend a few minutes at the Hilina Pali overlook. It is a quiet, remote spot, even though accessible by car. From the overlook you can see some of the trip route below on your left. Halapē is actually hidden behind the hump of Puʻu Kapukapu. Further along the coast are Keauhou and ʻApua Pts. Along the coast to the right are Punaluʻu and Nāʻālehu. In back is massive Mauna Loa.

Hilina Pali (cliff struck by wind) is a fault scarp, 12 miles long. The cliff formed when the coastal section suddenly dropped 1,500 feet. The Hilina fault system is still active, producing many small earthquakes.

Initially the route today descends Hilina Pali by a series of switchbacks. Watch your step as the rock underfoot is often loose. The remainder of the hike is over old *pāhoehoe* lava covered with grass. The trail is frequently rough and uneven, and the grass hides loose rock and pot holes. Again, watch your footing.

The trees on Hilina Pali with dark green, leathery leaves are lama. They were sacred to Laka, goddess of the hula. The Hawaiians used the hard, light colored wood in temple construction and in hula performances.

If you have time, climb Pu'u Kapukapu (regal hill). The ascent is harder than it looks because the approach is laced with cracks and collapsed lava tubes. From the top you can look straight down on Halapē. The view *mauka* (inland) reveals the massive slumping of this coastal section, producing Hilina, Makahanu, Pu'u'eo, Poliokeawe, and Hōlei Pali.

Halapē Shelter is located about $\frac{1}{4}$ mile inland near the base of Pu'u Kapukapu. The shelter has three sides, a sandy floor, and an open-air pit toilet nearby. As mentioned before, the shelter is not a good place to spend the night because its lava rock sides are home to cockroaches and mice.

Built into the back of the shelter is a water tank which is fed by rainfall collected on the roof. Boil, filter, or chemically treat the water. Don't waste it, especially in summer.

The shore campsites are along the line of palm trees to the left of the beach. If you have a choice, pick a site with a high rock wall to cut the wind. Don't pitch your tent right underneath a palm tree laden with coconuts!

Keep in mind that Halapē is located on a fault system where local earthquakes can generate destructive tsunami (sea waves). If you feel an earthquake, move to high ground immediately. In November 1975, a large earthquake struck the Big Island beneath the coast near Kalapana. The ground at Halapē suddenly dropped 10 feet. The resulting tsunami, 50 feet high, inundated the quiet lagoon fringed with palm trees and killed two campers. You can see some of the tree trunks still standing on the ocean side of the present cove.

Route Description

From the picnic shelter take the Hilina Pali Trail. As you face the ocean, it's the trail straight ahead, marked by a small wooden bulletin board. (The trail to the right, also marked by a bulletin board, is the Ka'ū Desert Trail, leading to Pepeiao Cabin.)

Descend gradually to the cliff edge and bear right along it.

Switch back twice and then go straight down as the slope angle eases momentarily.

Continue descending on a series of short switchbacks.

Cross an 'a'ā lava flow made up of rough, loose rock. Watch your footing.

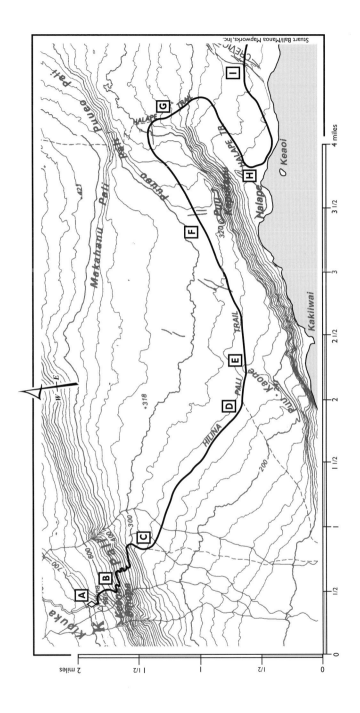

Pass a lama tree and an 'ōhi'a tree on the right.

Recross the 'a'ā flow several times on longer switchbacks (map point B).

On the right pass a lone lama tree. It's a shady spot to rest your legs.

Switch back one more time and then descend straight down to the base of the *pali*.

Reach a signed junction (map point C). Keep left on the Hilina Pali Trail to Halapē. (The trail to the right heads down to the coast at Ka'aha.)

Follow the *ahu* (cairns) across old *pāhoehoe* lava covered with grass.

Walk past a small grove of stunted 'ōhi'a trees.

The *pāhoehoe* becomes characteristically ropy in some areas.

Reach another signed junction (map point D). Again, keep left for Halapē. (The trail to the right connects with the Ka'aha Trail.)

Wind through scattered 'ōhi'a trees and lantana shrubs covered with morning glory vines.

Reach the top of Pu'u Kaone (map point E). Pu'u Kapukapu comes into view ahead.

Descend steeply, but briefly, and enter a grove of vine-covered koa haole trees.

Break out into the open and climb gradually.

Go through an opening in a rusted wire fence.

Traverse a rough section with steep humps and a series of cracks.

Gradually pass the top of Pu'u Kapukapu on the right (map point F).

Begin the descent to the coast.

The views open up dramatically. *Mauka* (inland) is Pu'u'eo Pali with Poliokeawe Pali behind. *Makai* (seaward), along the coast, is Keauhou Pt.

Descend more steeply. A fence line comes in on the right.

Cross the tip of an 'a'ā flow.

Shortly afterward, reach the signed junction with the Halapē Trail (map point G). Turn right on it toward the coast. (To the left the trail climbs *mauka* to the Kīpuka Nēnē Campground.)

Halapē finally comes into view. It's marked by a line of palm trees nestled under the cliff of Pu'u Kapukapu.

Descend steadily, winding through mounds and large chunks of *pāhoehoe*. There are switchbacks on the steeper sections.

Bear right to parallel the coast.

Reach Halapē Shelter (elev. 40 ft) (map point H) and the junction with the Puna Coast Trail.

Take the unmarked path in front of the shelter to the shore. The campsites are located to the left of a small white sand beach.

DAY TWO— Layover at Halapē

There are lots of possibilities for today. Sunbathe on the beach. Explore the tide pools. Go swimming or snorkeling in the cove. I have even seen an occasional surfer there!

For a short hike, walk west along the coast to Boulder Bay at the very foot of Pu'u Kapukapu. Along the way are anchialine ponds in the deep lava cracks. The water in the ponds is brackish, fed by the tide, rainfall, and seepage. Just before reaching the bay is a *kōnane* playing board, etched into the rock. *Kōnane* is an ancient Hawaiian game similar to checkers. The low-lying shrub nearby is 'ilima papa, a native with heart-shaped leaves. The Hawaiians strung the orange flowers to make leis for special occasions.

For a longer day hike, head east along the Puna Coast Trail to Keauhou. That is the route out tomorrow, but you may not have time to explore it then. The snorkeling at Keauhou is superb with plenty of color-ful reef fish and coral. The best area is in the cove on the Halapē side of the point. The fresh water entering the ocean there does make for some temperature fluctuation and fuzzy viewing, however.

Perhaps the best option of all, especially in the afternoon, is to hang around Halapē and do absolutely nothing. Sit underneath a palm tree. Watch the waves. Take a nap. Think big thoughts. Whatever.

Halapē literally means crushed and missing. The strong winds here would completely bury gourds growing near the beach. People passing by would not see them and thus miss them.

DAY THREE—Halapē to Pu'uloa

Length: 11.3 mi

Elev. Gain: 100 ft

The Puna Coast Trail roughly follows the route of the historic Ka'ū-Puna Trail. Hawaiian *ali'i* (chiefs), commoners, and tax collectors used the trail to travel between *ahupua'a* (land divisions). Their boundaries were marked by *ahu* (rock altars) on which the carved image of a *pua'a* (pig) was placed annually to advise people that taxes were due.

The hike today is not difficult, but the route is long, so start early. The coast trail crosses miles and miles of old and new lava. On the way are two worthwhile side trips, to Keauhou and 'Āpua Pts.

To get to Keauhou (new era or current), take the side trail near the shelter. At the shore, turn right to reach the cove with great snorkeling. Keep left to get to the site of Keauhou landing. It is marked by an old water tank and rock-walled corrals. In the 1800s the landing was used to ship cattle to the other islands. Keauhou is also the site of an ancient village destroyed by a tsunami in 1868.

If you have time, branch off the coast trail to 'Āpua (fish basket) Pt., an extraordinarily wild and windy spot. It is one of the few nesting areas of the endangered Hawksbill turtle. 'Āpua is also the site of an ancient village swept away by the 1868 tsunami. To regain the main trail, walk along the rocky beach and then cut back *mauka* through the naupaka shrubs.

After passing 'Āpua Pt., the trail hugs the coast for over a mile. There is some greenery here, in contrast to the black lava and blue ocean. The low-lying succulent shrub is naupaka kahakai. Its flowers are white with purple streaks and appear half formed. Less common is 'ohai, a spreading shrub with elliptic leaflets and scarlet winged and clawed flowers.

The series of new lava flows you cross all came from Mauna Ulu (growing mountain), a volcanic shield about seven miles inland. On their way to the ocean the flows cut Chain of Craters Rd. and plunged spectacularly over Hōlei Pali. The 1971 flow covered the site of the ancient village of Kealakomo (the entrance path). You can see Mauna Ulu on the Nāpau Crater trip.

If you have any energy left at all after reaching the Pu'uloa trailhead, take the one mile walk to the petroglyphs. The site has hundreds of figures carved into the *pāhoehoe* lava.

Route Description

Take the shore path along the line of palm trees and rock-walled campsites.

At the last site bear right on the Puna Coast Trail, heading east. It is marked by *ahu* topped with white coral for easier viewing. (To the left the trail leads back to the shelter.)

Climb very gradually through grass on old *pāhoehoe*. Turn around for a last view of Halapē. In back is Nāli'ikakani Pt. and the coast to Nā'ālehu.

Pass some rolls of fence wire and a fishing regulation sign.

Reach the edge of a small *pali* and descend it on a well-crafted rock staircase (map point I). The steep cliff in the distance to the left is Hōlei Pali.

Walk through scrub koa haole trees.

Climb gradually, again on grass-covered *pāhoehoe*.

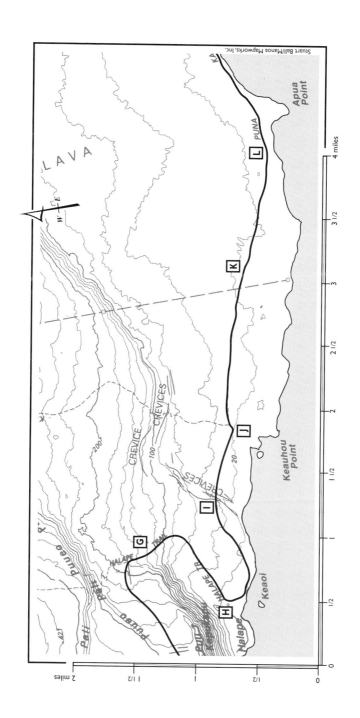

LAVA

Puuo Pali

Puuo Pali

Pihau Pali

HALAPE TRAIL

Keauhou Trail

HALAPE TR

Halape

CREVICE

CREVICES

CREVICES

100

200

20

G

H

I

J

K

L

PUNA

KA

Keaoi

Keauhou
Point

Apua
Point

N
W E
S

Stuart Ball/Manoa Mapworks, Inc.

0   1/2   1   1 1/2   2 1/2   3   3 1/2   4 miles

0   1/2   1   1 1/2   2 miles

Reach a signed junction (map point J). Continue straight on the coast trail. (To the right, a side trail leads down to Keauhou Pt. and Landing.)

Almost immediately the trail splits. Keep right on the main trail. (The side trail to the left leads to Keauhou Shelter, which has a water tank and an open-air pit toilet.)

Shortly afterward reach a second signed junction. Continue straight on the Puna Coast Trail. (To the left, the Keauhou Trail heads *mauka* to Chain of Craters Rd.)

Walk on old *pāhoehoe* covered with grass.

Traverse a more recent flow of black *pāhoehoe*.

Return to the old well-worn *pāhoehoe* covered with grass.

Cross a finger of shiny black lava, part of the 1973 flow from Mauna Ulu (map point K).

Resume walking on grass-covered *pāhoehoe*.

Traverse a wide section of new black lava from the 1973 flow.

Jog right, toward the coast, and then left paralleling it.

Climb gradually. 'Āpua Pt. with its palm trees comes into view. The trade winds pick up.

The trail angles toward the coast while descending very gradually.

Reach an unmarked junction (map point L). Keep left on the main trail which crosses an older flow. (The less distinct trail to the right on the 1973 flow leads to 'Āpua Pt. The point has a campsite and a compost toilet, but no water.)

Reach the coast on the far side of 'Āpua Pt.

Cross a flat sandy area covered with beach naupaka.

Traverse the 1969 flow from Mauna Ulu (map point M). The lava is *'a'ā*, rough and clinkery, but a welcome change from the acres of *pāhoehoe*.

Walk on black sand through beach naupaka with some 'ohai. On the right, just off the trail, is a *kōnane* playing board etched into the rock.

Reach a large rock-wall corral and go around it to the right.

Cross old *pāhoehoe* covered with naupaka and grass.

The trail gradually angles away from the coast.

Traverse the lumpy 1970 flow from Mauna Ulu (map point N).

Return to old *pāhoehoe* covered with grass.

On the right pass an oval rock marker for fishermen.

Cross the wide 1971 flow from Mauna Ulu (map point O). The trail winds through a rough sea of billowy lava.

Traverse the shiny 1972 flow, also from Mauna Ulu (map point P). On

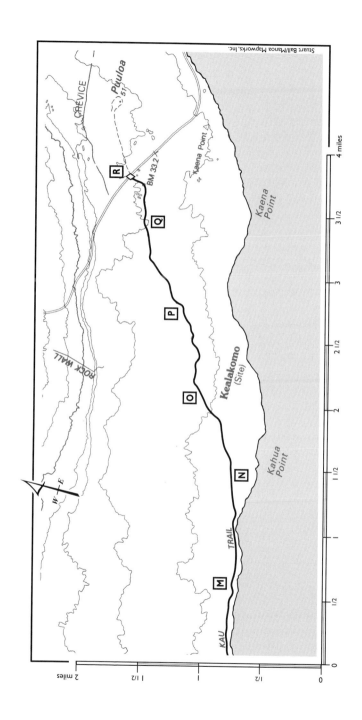

the right is a view of Kahue Pt. The far side of the flow is broken and jumbled up.

Cross the remnants of an old grass-covered flow.

Traverse some more of the humpy 1972 flow (map point Q). (And you thought you were done with it!)

Cross one last stretch of old grass-covered *pāhoehoe*.

Reach Chain of Craters Rd. at the Pu'uloa petroglyphs turnout (elev. 140 ft) (map point R).

Options

There are several variations of this trip. You can do the route in reverse if you don't mind climbing Hilina Pali. You can return the way you came in if you only have one car and don't want to hitchhike. You can do the trip in two days, but you'll regret not spending the extra day at Halapē.

Groups with 4 to 5 days to spare have two options. Spend the additional days relaxing and exploring at Halapē, or combine the Ka'aha and Halapē trips. For the first two days, follow the route to Ka'aha. On the third day take the connector trail to the Hilina Pali Trail and Halapē.

Ka'aha and Halapē are similar trips. If you can only do one, choose Halapē for its white sand beach and shady palm trees. Halapē can get crowded, however, especially on weekends. If you want solitude, pick Ka'aha.

There are two other routes to Halapē, the Keauhou Trail and the Halapē Trail. The latter is the most direct and scenic route. The trail starts from Kīpuka Nēnē Campground, descends through Kīpuka Papālinamoku and down Hilina and Pu'u'eo Pali to Halapē in 7.2 miles. However, the National Park Service closes the campground and the upper section of the Halapē Trail from November through April each year during the breeding season of the nēnē goose. If you plan to do the trip in summer, by all means take the Halapē Trail.

The Keauhou Trail is a longer and perhaps less scenic route to Halapē. The trail starts from Chain of Craters Rd. and descends Poliokeawe Pali to Keauhou in 6.8 miles. At the shelter there, turn right on the Puna Coast Trail for another 1.6 miles to reach Halapē.

2. Ka'aha

Type:	Shoreline
Length:	3 days, 14.6 mi loop
Elev. Gain/Loss:	2,300/2,300 ft
Difficulty:	Medium
Location:	Hawai'i (the Big Island): Hawai'i Volcanoes National Park
Topo Map:	Ka'ū Desert, Nāli'ikakani Pt

Highlights

This trip leads down to Ka'aha, an oasis along the stark, windswept Ka'ū coast. Along the way you see fault systems, lava tubes, sea arches, and *kīpuka*, which are islands of vegetation surrounded by newer lava flows. The trip ends with a spectacular climb of Hilina Pali, a 1,500-foot-high cliff.

Planning

Call or write the National Park for a brochure, trail map, and camping information. The visitor center phone number is (808) 967–7311, and the address is Superintendent, Hawai'i Volcanoes National Park, HI 96718.

Winter (November–April) is the best time of year to take this trip. The temperature then is cooler, and the sun less intense. If you must do the trip in summer, use plenty of sunscreen and drink lots of water. The only shade along the coast is in the Ka'aha Shelter.

Bring a tent as both Pepeiao Cabin and Ka'aha Shelter are overrun with cockroaches and mice at night. Take a light sleeping bag or liner as the nights can be chilly, especially in winter. *Tabis* (Japanese reef walkers) with their fuzzy bottoms are perfect for exploring the slippery, rocky shoreline.

If possible, plan to arrive on the Big Island at Hilo. The driving instructions below start from the Hilo Airport. All major rental car firms have booths there.

There is a public bus, known as Hele-on, from Hilo to the National Park once a day. Call the Hawai'i County Transit System at (808) 935–8241 for the current schedule.

If you are arriving at Keāhole Airport near Kailua (Kona), you have a longer drive. Exit Keāhole Airport and turn right on Queen Ka'ahumanu

Hwy (Rte 19) to Kailua (Kona). There, pick up Hawai'i Belt Rd. (Rte 11) and follow it around the southern tip of the island to the National Park. The distance to the trailhead is 118 miles and the driving time, about 3 ¼ hours.

Coleman fuel (white gas) is available at the 7-Eleven stores in Hilo, Hirano Store in Glenwood, and Volcano Store in Volcano. All three have some food items. For a wider selection stop at Safeway in the Prince Kūhiō Plaza or KTA Super Stores. Both are along Kanoelehua Ave. on the way out of Hilo.

Once in the park stop at the Kīlauea Visitor Center to get a back-country permit. The center is open from 7:30 A.M. to 4:45 P.M. seven days a week. Check on the water supply at the cabin and the shelter. Fill your water bottles for the first day as there is no water available at the trailhead.

Trailhead Directions

Distance: (Hilo Airport to Hilina Pali trailhead)—46 mi

Driving Time: 1 ½ hr

Exit Hilo Airport on Airport Rd.

At the first traffic light, turn left on Kanoelehua Ave. (Rte 11) to Volcano.

Kanoelehua Ave. becomes Hawai'i Belt Rd. (still Rte 11).

Just past Kea'au, the road narrows to two lanes.

Ascend gradually, passing the villages of Kurtistown, Mountain View, and Glenwood.

Pass turnoffs to Volcano village on the right.

Enter Hawai'i Volcanoes National Park.

Shortly afterward, turn left at the sign for the park entrance.

Pay the fee at the entrance station.

Stop at Kīlauea Visitor Center on the right (elev. 3,974 ft). There, get a backcountry permit for the trip and ask about current trail conditions. Remember to fill your water bottles.

Drive back toward the entrance station.

Just before reaching it, turn right on Crater Rim Dr.

Turn left at the stop sign.

Pass Kīlauea Iki overlook on the right and Thurston (Nāhuku) lava tube on the left.

Wind through a tree fern and 'ōhi'a forest.

Pass the turnoff to Pu'u Pua'i on the right.

At the next intersection turn left on Chain of Craters Rd.

Pass turnoffs to Puhimau Crater on the left and Ko'oko'olau Crater on the right.

Turn right on Hilina Pali Rd.

Pass Kīpuka Nēnē campground on the left.

Reach the end of the road at Hilina Pali overlook (elev. 2,280 ft) (map point A). Park in the lot next to the picnic shelter.

DAY ONE—Hilina Pali overlook to Kīpuka Pepeiao

Length: 4.8 mi

Elev. Loss: 600 ft

The hike today is short and mostly downhill so spend some time at the Hilina Pali overlook. It is a quiet, remote spot, even though accessible by car. From the overlook you can see much of the Ka'ū coast. To the left are Keauhou and 'Āpua Pts. Halapē is hidden behind Pu'u Kapukapu. To the right along the coast are Punalu'u and Nā'ālehu. In back is massive Mauna Loa.

Hilina Pali (cliff struck by wind) is a fault scarp, 12 miles long. The cliff formed when the coastal section suddenly dropped 1,500 feet. The Hilina fault system is still active, producing many small earthquakes.

The route today parallels the fault system through Kīpuka 'Āhiu (wild *kīpuka*) and Kīpuka Pepeiao (ear *kīpuka*). *Kīpuka* are islands of vegetation on old lava surrounded by newer barren flows. The vegetation is not lush here because of the high temperatures coupled with low rainfall. Predominating are scrub 'ōhi'a trees, pūkiawe, and grass. 'Ōhi'a colonizes new flows and reaches maturity on older flows such as these. Look for the clusters of delicate red flowers. Pūkiawe is the woody shrub with narrow, rigid leaves and small white, pink, or red fruits. Along the trail before the cabin are bamboo orchids with purple and yellow flowers.

Pepeiao Cabin has three beds, a table, chairs, and a metal locker for food storage. Nearby is a pit toilet. As mentioned earlier, the cabin is not a good place to spend the night as it is overrun with cockroaches and mice. Pitch your tent on a grassy spot near the cabin.

On the side of the cabin is a water tank that is fed by rainfall collected on the roof. Boil, filter, or chemically treat the water. Don't waste it, especially in summer.

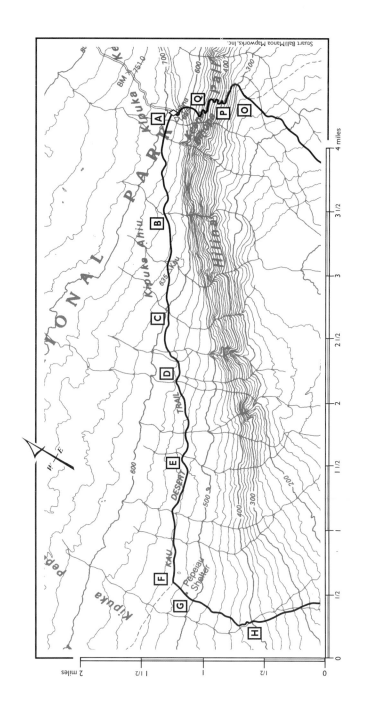

If you still have some time and energy left after reaching the cabin, explore further along the Ka'ū Desert Trail. If you don't, peruse the cabin log book for trail facts, impressions, jokes, and other commentary.

Route Description

From the picnic shelter take the Ka'ū Desert Trail. As you face the ocean, it's the trail on the right, marked by a small wooden bulletin board. (The trail straight ahead, also marked by a bulletin board, is the Hilina Pali Trail. It descends the *pali* to the coast and is the return portion of this loop trip.)

Walk along the top of Hilina Pali through grass, scattered 'ōhi'a trees, and pūkiawe. Piles of rock, called *ahu* (cairns), mark the trail. There are good views along the coast toward Punalu'u and Nā'ālehu.

Cross several dry stream beds.

Descend gradually through open grass land.

Cross a small watercourse and then a large rocky one (map point B).

Climb briefly and then resume the leisurely descent toward a scrub 'ōhi'a forest.

Cross several more stream beds, one very rocky.

Enter the forest (map point C). The lava underfoot is old *pāhoehoe* with the characteristic ropy appearance.

The trees gradually thin out.

Descend and climb out of a deep watercourse lined with 'ōhi'a (map point D).

Negotiate old, but still rough, *'a'ā* lava with ridges paralleling the flow.

Cross a newer *pāhoehoe* flow with smooth grey lava.

Traverse a wide old *'a'ā* flow, deeply cut by a series of rocky stream beds.

Descend briefly and cross a sandy wash that branches upstream (map point E).

Cross another large watercourse in a grassy bowl-shaped area.

Traverse a level section with scattered 'ōhi'a.

Pass an open grassy area on the right.

Climb imperceptively to a knoll with a view of the coastline and Pepeiao Cabin below.

Reach a signed junction (map point F). Turn left on to the Ka'aha Trail. (To the right the Ka'ū Desert Trail leads to Mauna Iki, the Footprints Exhibit, and Route 11.)

Descend briefly to reach Pepeiao Cabin and campsite (elev. 1,680 ft) (map point G).

DAY TWO—Kīpuka Pepeiao to Ka'aha

Length: 6 mi

Elev. Loss: 1,700 ft

The route today is all downhill, but the walking is tougher than it looks on the map. The trail is rough, uneven, and steep in spots. There are lots of little ups and downs, especially along the coast. Before reaching Kūkala'ula Pali (red proclamation cliff), you pass the last 'ōhi'a tree. From there on it's all lava, wind, sun, sand, and sea.

Nāpu'uonā'elemākule (hills of the old men) is a good spot for lunch or break. Explore the rocky beach and sea arches there. Remember the adage—never turn your back on the ocean.

Just along the coast is an area known as 'Opihinehe. According to legend, it was forbidden to rattle 'opihi shells there. If you did, a ghost asked another ghost "seaward or inland?" Depending on the answer, you then drowned or had a fatal accident on land. 'Opihi are the local limpets that cling to rocks continuously washed by waves. Their shells are conical, black, and deeply grooved.

After 'Opihinehe the trail heads inland and then roughly parallels the coast. If you wish, stay along the coast for a while longer. You can always cut back *mauka* (inland) to rejoin the main trail to Ka'aha.

Ka'aha (the assembly) stands out as the only patch of green along the otherwise barren coast. Fresh water seeping close to the surface of the lava enters the ocean here. The green is mostly naupaka kahakai, a spreading, succulent shrub. Its flowers are white with purple streaks and appear half formed.

Ka'aha Shelter is located about ¼ mile inland at the foot of a small *pali* (cliff). The shelter has three sides, a sandy floor, and a pit toilet nearby. As mentioned before, the shelter is not a good place to spend the night because its lava rock sides are home to cockroaches and mice. Near the shelter are several tent sites with rock-wall windbreaks.

Built into the back of the shelter is a water tank that is fed by rainfall collected on the roof. Boil, filter, or chemically treat the water. Don't waste it, especially in summer.

After setting up camp, take the trail from the shelter down to the shore. The trail ends at a small cove with the beginnings of a black sand beach. Go swimming or snorkeling; explore the tide pools; walk along the coast toward Kālu'e (hanging loose); or just sit on the beach and take in the wild beauty of the area.

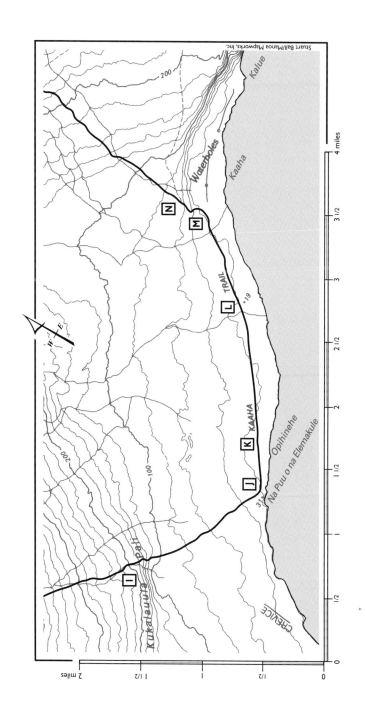

The snorkeling at Ka'aha is good, but not great. The fresh water entering the cove makes for some temperature fluctuations and fuzzy viewing. There are some colorful coral and a good variety of reef fish. The best area is the ocean side of the cove near the wave break.

Route Description

From the front of the cabin continue down toward the coast on the Ka'aha Trail. (The mileage sign is mismarked Kālu'e Trail.)

Descend gradually on an old *pāhoehoe* flow covered with grass and scattered 'ōhi'a.

Go along a sandy wash (map point H).

Jog left and then right, down a tiny *pali*.

Rejoin the dry watercourse.

Reach a prominent *ahu* where you get the first good view of the coast. To the left is Kālu'e, Halapē, and Keauhou with 'Āpua Pt. in the distance. Pu'u Kaone is the cliff above Kālu'e, and Pu'u Kapukapu is the cone above Halapē. Just down the trail the coastline on the right opens up.

Continue the descent, following small, sometimes sandy, washes. Look left for a spectacular view along Hilina Pali.

Reach the top of Kūkala'ula Pali (map point I) and bear left along it.

Descend steeply along the face of the *pali*. There are no switchbacks. Watch your footing as the rock is loose. Watch for the *ahu* as they blend in with the landscape when going downhill.

Just before reaching the base of the cliff, turn right, straight down.

At the bottom veer right and then back left toward the coast.

Descend very gradually over old *pāhoehoe,* covered sparsely with grass.

Jog left and then right to go around a large crack.

As the coast nears, the lava becomes bare and very black.

Reach the ocean at a small, sandy-colored hill, known as Nāpu-'uonā'elemākule (map point J). On either side of the hill are sea arches with a secluded rocky beach in between.

Turn left along the coast toward Ka'aha.

Walk through an area called 'Opihinehe (map point K).

Cross a flat section covered with black sand.

Traverse a long stretch of billowy *pāhoehoe* broken into small humps. Again, the *ahu* blend in with the lava background. Some are topped with white coral or fishing floats to make them easier to see.

Bear left inland to skirt a flat sandy area (map point L).

Cross black sand covered with small rocks.

Resume hiking up, down, and around humpy *pāhoehoe* (groan!).
Traverse a grassy, extremely rough lava flow. Watch closely for the *ahu*.
Reach the Ka'aha Shelter and camp12site (elev. 80 ft) (map point M).

DAY THREE—Ka'aha to Hilina Pali overlook

Length: 3.8 mi

Elev. Gain: 2,300 ft

Today you gain back all the elevation you lost on the previous two days. At least the route is short and has switchbacks on the steep climb up Hilina Pali. Watch your footing constantly there.

If you wish, start very early in the morning to beat the heat. Otherwise, wait until after lunch. The initial walking is hot, but late afternoon usually brings strong trade winds and heavy cloud buildup *mauka* (inland). The air then becomes much cooler for the final climb up the *pali*. Besides, by starting late, you have the morning to snorkel in the cove or walk the coast.

If you like caves, explore some of the lava tubes along the trail. Take a flashlight and extra batteries. Once inside, watch your head; the ceilings are often low and jagged. When you are well away from the entrance, turn off your flashlight to get a new meaning for the word dark. While inside the tube, don't spend too much time thinking about earthquakes!

Lava tubes are usually formed in *pāhoehoe* flows that are confined, such as in a gully. The top and edges of the flow cool and crust over. The lava inside continues to flow through the resulting tunnel. Eventually, the flow diminishes and stops, leaving a tube.

Route Description

From the shelter walk past the toilet, keeping it on the right.

Almost immediately, turn right on to the Ka'aha Trail.

Angle to the right, up a short, but steep, *pali*.

At the top of the *pali*, bear left *mauka*.

Pass the entrance to a lava tube on the right.

Reach a signed junction (map point N). Keep left on the Ka'aha Trail. (The trail to the right heads along the coast to Halapē.)

Ascend gradually on old *pāhoehoe* covered with grass. Follow the *ahu* extending into the distance.

Bear right in a parallel with Hilina Pali.

Gradually work left toward the base of the *pali*. The climb becomes steeper.

Reach a signed junction (map point O) with the Hilina Pali Trail. Turn left on it toward the *pali*. (To the right the trail leads down to Halapē on the coast.)

Climb Hilina Pali on a series of 22 switchbacks. (Easier said than done!) There are several highlights. At 2, a lone tree provides some shade for a break. Between 3 and 5, you will cross an ‘a‘ā flow. Watch your footing on the loose rock. After 5 (map point P), there is a view of Ka‘aha way below in the distance. Between 8 and 9, you will cross an ‘a‘ā flow again. After 19 (map point Q), the slope angle decreases markedly, and the trail goes straight up. At 20, resume switchbacking.

Shortly after switchback 22, reach Hilina Pali overlook and picnic shelter (elev. 2,280 ft) (map point A).

Options

There are a few variations of this trip, none as attractive as the route described. You can, of course, do the loop clockwise, visiting the coast first and then the *kīpuka*. Somehow the reverse seems more appealing.

For a longer first day, start hiking from the Ka‘ū Desert trailhead on Route 11. Take the Mauna Iki Trail past the Footprints Exhibit. Turn right on the Ka‘ū Desert Trail to Pepeiao Cabin. That option adds 4.3 miles to the first day for a total of 9.1 miles. You either need two cars or else have to do some hitchhiking.

Groups with limited time can make a two-day trip to the coast. Descend Hilina Pali to Ka‘aha on the first day and return the same way on the second. That route is only 3.8 miles one way so you should have some time to explore the shoreline. It's a shame to miss Kīpuka Pepeiao, though.

Novice backpackers can spend one night at Pepeiao Cabin and then return the next day. That short trip provides a good introduction to camping in Volcanoes National Park.

Parties with 4 to 5 days to spare can combine the Ka‘aha and Halapē trips. From Ka‘aha take the connector trail to the Hilina Pali Trail and Halapē. Follow the *ahu* religiously as that trail is little used and overgrown.

Ka‘aha and Halapē are similar trips. Halapē is deservedly more popular because of its white sand beach and shady palm trees. If, however, you want solitude, stick with Ka‘aha.

3. Mauna Loa

Type:	Mountain
Length:	3–6 days, 38.2 mi round trip
Elev. Gain/Loss:	6,600/6,600 ft
Difficulty:	High
Location:	Hawaiʻi (the Big Island): Hawaiʻi Volcanoes National Park
Topo Map:	Kīpuka Pakēkakē, Puʻu ʻUlaʻula, Kokoʻolau, Mauna Loa

Highlights

Mauna Loa (long mountain) is the largest volcano in the world. This trip climbs to its summit (elev. 13,679 ft) following the northeast rift zone. Along the way you see deep pit craters, colorful spatter cones, and acres and acres of barren lava. The summit cabin overlooks Mokuʻāweoweo, a huge desolate crater with steaming vents and fissures.

Planning

Call or write the National Park for a brochure, trail map, and camping information. The visitor center phone number is (808) 967–7311, and the address is Superintendent, Hawaiʻi Volcanoes National Park, HI 96718.

Summer (May–August) is the best time of year to take this trip. The days are long, and the weather is usually settled. You can do the trip in winter (December–March). The days, however, are shorter, and snow is more common then. A storm can blanket the trail at higher elevation with several inches or feet of snow. It usually lingers, however, only in cracks and on north-facing slopes.

Be prepared for huge temperature swings. At night the thermometer drops to the thirties in summer and twenties in winter. Midday temperatures range from 50 to 80 degrees depending on the elevation. Wind chill can make those temperatures much lower.

Bring a three-season sleeping bag and four layers of clothing. The outer layer should protect you from wind, rain, and snow. Include warm gloves or mittens and a hat or balaclava. Bring at least one extra day of food in case a snowstorm strands you in one of the cabins. No tent is required.

If possible, plan to arrive on the Big Island at Hilo. The driving instructions below start from the Hilo Airport. All major rental car firms have booths there.

There is a public bus, known as Hele-on, from Hilo to the National Park once a day. Call the Hawai'i County Transit System at (808) 935–8241 for the current schedule.

If you are arriving at Keāhole Airport near Kailua (Kona), you have a longer drive. Exit Keāhole Airport and turn right on Queen Ka'ahumanu Hwy (Rte 19) to Kailua (Kona). There, pick up Hawai'i Belt Rd. (Rte 11) and follow it around the southern tip of the island to the National Park. The distance to the trailhead is 118 miles and the driving time, about 3 ¼ hours.

Coleman fuel (white gas) is available at the 7-Eleven stores in Hilo, Hirano Store in Glenwood, and Volcano Store in Volcano. All three have some food items. For a wider selection stop at Safeway in the Prince Kūhiō Plaza or KTA Super Stores. Both are along Kanoelehua Ave. on the way out of Hilo.

Once in the park stop at the Kīlauea Visitor Center to get a back-country permit. The center is open from 7:30 A.M. to 4:45 P.M. seven days a week. Check on the water supply at the cabins. Fill your water bottles for the first day as there is no water available at the trailhead.

At the visitor center look for the *Mauna Loa Trail Guide* by Lisa Petersen. It's an inexpensive pamphlet crammed with information about the trail and its history, and the mountain and its geology.

Finally, take this trip seriously. It has nothing in common with beaches, palm trees, and the rest of tourist Hawai'i. This is alpine hiking with 2 to 5 nights spent above 10,000 feet. Altitude sickness is common. Its effects are, at best, miserable and, at worst, life threatening. Unless you've backpacked in California or Colorado, you have probably never experienced anything like this before.

Trailhead Directions

Distance: (Hilo Airport to Mauna Loa trailhead)—43 mi

Driving Time: 1 ½ hr

Exit Hilo Airport on Airport Rd.

At the first traffic light, turn left on Kanoelehua Ave. (Rte 11) to Volcano.

Kanoelehua Ave. becomes Hawai'i Belt Rd. (still Rte 11).

Just past Kea'au, the road narrows to two lanes.

Ascend gradually, passing the villages of Kurtistown, Mountain View, and Glenwood.

Pass turnoffs to Volcano village on the right.

Enter Hawai'i Volcanoes National Park.

Shortly afterward, turn left at the sign for the park entrance.

Pay the fee at the entrance station.

Stop at Kīlauea Visitor Center on the right (elev. 3,974 ft). There, get a backcountry permit for Mauna Loa and ask about current trail conditions. Remember to fill your water bottles.

Drive back through the entrance station.

Turn left on Hawai'i Belt Rd. (Rte 11).

On the right pass a turnoff to Volcano golf course.

At the next intersection turn right on Mauna Loa Rd.

Pass Kīpuka Paulu (Bird Park) on the right.

Drive through Kīpuka Kī, a special ecological study area.

Cross two cattle guards.

Cross the Ke'āmoku flow, made up of old 'a'ā lava.

Climb gradually through a lovely koa-'ōhi'a forest in Kīpuka Kulalio.

Reach the end of the road at Mauna Loa lookout (elev. 6,662 ft) (map point A). Park your car in the small lot next to the picnic shelter.

DAY ONE—Mauna Loa lookout to Pu'u 'Ula'ula

Length: 7.5 mi

Elev. Gain: 3,400 ft

Get an early start so you can take it easy on the trail. Stretch the hike out all day to lessen the strain on your body from the increased altitude. Take frequent breaks and drink plenty of water. The climbing is steady, but not steep. The path is well worn, even smooth in spots, because the route lies over old lava.

The Mauna Loa Trail was built in 1915 by a company of black soldiers in the U.S. Army. The trail originally started at the old Volcano Observatory near Volcano House and the visitor center. The lower section roughly followed the route you now drive to the trailhead. Parts of the original upper section have been rerouted, sometimes because of new lava flows.

The first stretch of the present day Mauna Loa Trail passes through very old native dry-land forest dominated by koa and 'ōhi'a trees. 'Ōhi'a colonizes recent lava flows and reaches maturity on older ones. The delicate red flowers grow in clusters and attract native birds, such as 'apapane and 'i'iwi.

Koa trees have sickle-shaped leaves and small yellow flowers. The Hawaiians used the wood for canoes, surfboards, and spears. Also along the trail is an occasional māmane tree with soft pinnate (featherlike) leaves and yellow, winged flowers. Like the 'ōhi'a, its nectar attracts a variety of native birds.

As the trail begins climbing, the trees start to thin. More in evidence are the shrubs pūkiawe, 'a'ali'i, and 'ōhelo. Pūkiawe has narrow, rigid leaves and small white, pink, or red fruits. 'A'ali'i has shiny green leaves and red seed capsules. 'Ōhelo has thin leaves and red or purple berries, which are delicious.

Above 9,000 feet many people start to feel the altitude. If you have a headache, nausea, or difficulty breathing, slow your pace. Breathe deeply and rest often. Keep plodding one step at a time and watch Pu'u 'Ula'ula slowly get bigger.

Pu'u 'Ula'ula (red hill) is a spatter cone formed by an eruption about 8,500 years ago. It is the first and oldest cone you walk by on this trip. Weathering through the years has oxidized the iron in the lava, turning it rusty red.

The U.S. Army built the Pu'u 'Ula'ula Rest House in 1915. The cabin has eight bunks, a table, chairs, and an area for cooking. There are extra mattresses so you can sleep on the floor or the porch if all the bunks are filled. Outside the cabin are two pit toilets and a water tank, which is fed by rainfall from the roof. Boil, filter, or chemically treat the water.

After dinner, take the short climb to the top of Pu'u 'Ula'ula. At sunset you can sometimes see the image of Mauna Loa projected on the clouds and sky to the east. Across the saddle to the north is Mauna Kea (white mountain), a dormant volcano and the highest point in the state at 13,796 feet. You can see several observatories clustered near its summit. Behind and to the left of Mauna Kea is Haleakalā (house of the sun) on the island of Maui. To the northeast are the lights of Hilo town way below in the distance. In June you can see the Southern Cross low in the sky to the south.

Route Description

The Mauna Loa Trail starts in back of the parking lot.

Pass a pit toilet on the left and a wooden bulletin board with trail information on the right.

Enter a grove of koa trees.

Contour across the slope through native dry-land forest. The vegetation includes 'ōhi'a, 'ōhelo, pūkiawe, 'a'ali'i, and an occasional māmane. Enjoy the greenery while it lasts!

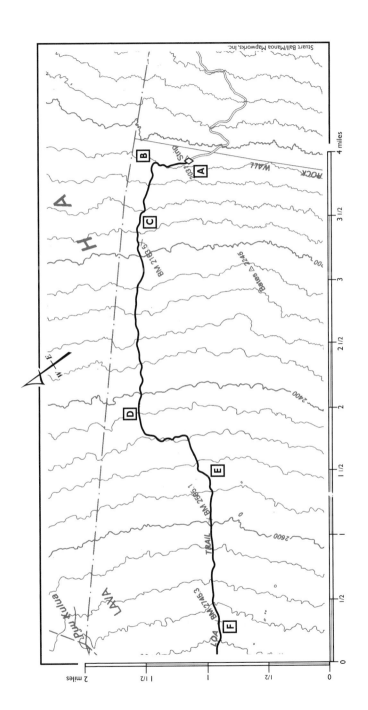

On the right are views of Kīlauea Crater, Halemaʻumaʻu fire pit, and the rest of the Volcano area.

Bear left upslope on old reddish *pāhoehoe* lava (map point B). The trail is marked by piles of rock, called *ahu*.

Go through a wooden gate. Close it behind you to keep cattle and feral goats and pigs out of the lower section of the park.

Ascend gradually through scattered ʻōhiʻa trees. Work left or right to avoid steeper sections.

The *pāhoehoe* lava underfoot becomes a field of mounds. On the right is the massive Keʻāmoku flow, consisting of prehistoric *ʻaʻā* lava.

Reach the 7,000-foot elevation marker (map point C).

The vegetation gradually thins. Way below on the right is Kūlani cone, an old forested cinder cone.

The top of Mauna Loa opens up on the left.

Reach the 8,000-foot elevation marker (map point D).

Shortly afterward, pass a lone ʻōhiʻa next to the trail. The tree makes a shady rest spot.

Just beyond the tree, turn left and contour across the slope. The trail is sandy in spots and crosses some *ʻaʻā* lava for the first time.

Pass the last tree, a bushy ʻōhiʻa on the left. ʻŌhelo, pūkiawe, and ʻaʻaliʻi still dot the landscape.

Resume climbing on very humpy *pāhoehoe*.

Cross a prehistoric *ʻaʻā* flow with somewhat thicker vegetation. The trail is very rough; watch your footing on the loose rock.

Switch to smooth *pāhoehoe*. The trail is grooved into the lava.

Angle left and across a weathered *ʻaʻā* flow (map point E). ʻŌhelo is now the only remaining green among the brown and black lava.

Return to the lovely smooth *pāhoehoe* and the sunken trail.

Parallel a large lava tube. In places the tube has collapsed forming a trench or series of pits.

Climb more steeply to reach the top of a rise. From there you can first see Puʻu ʻUlaʻula, today's destination. It's the prominent red cone in the distance upslope. To the right is Puʻu Kūluā, a black prehistoric spatter cone. Behind and near the coast is Puʻu ʻŌʻo, a recently active vent and cone of Kīlauea Volcano.

On the left pass a large pit, part of the collapsed lava tube.

Reach the 9,000-foot elevation marker (map point F).

Continue to follow the lava tube, crossing it several times.

Gradually angle left across a wide, weathered *pāhoehoe* flow, leaving the lava tube behind (map point G).

Keep working left and up, across a broad '*a'ā* flow. Pass the last of the 'ōhelo.

Switch back to *pāhoehoe* and begin climbing straight up toward Pu'u 'Ula'ula.

Wind through red-brown '*a'ā* and cinders from Pu'u 'Ula'ula.

Climb steadily around the left side of the cone.

Reach the Pu'u 'Ula'ula Rest House (elev. 10,035 ft) (map point H).

DAY TWO—Layover at Pu'u 'Ula'ula

If you have no symptoms of altitude sickness, continue up the mountain today. If, however, you still have a headache, nausea, and/or irregular breathing, spend the day resting at Pu'u 'Ula'ula. Eat sparingly, but drink plenty of water.

The day passes surprisingly quickly. Read a book or the cabin log. Its entries are often informative, sometimes humorous, and occasionally inane. If you feel like it, take a short hike to stretch your legs. Walk up or down the trail or explore the nearby cones to the northeast. In the late afternoon, sit on the cabin porch and enjoy the warmth of the sun.

About a mile below Pu'u 'Ula'ula to the northeast lies the main vent of the 1984 eruption. Lava poured from the vent for 21 days and flowed 17 miles toward Hilo. The eruption actually started in the summit crater, Moku'āweoweo, on March 25. A line of fountains, called a curtain of fire, opened up along a fissure and covered the crater floor with new lava. The magma then moved underground down the northeast rift zone toward Pu'u 'Ula'ula. Curtains of fire appeared between North Pit and Pōhaku Hanalei and between Dewey Cone and Pukauahi. Those cones and craters, as well as the 1984 lava, will become very familiar to you tomorrow as you trudge up the rift zone.

DAY THREE—Pu'u 'Ula'ula to Mauna Loa Cabin

Length: 11.6 mi

Elev. Gain: 3,200 ft

Start very early today because you are going to need every hour of daylight. The thin air makes for slow walking even though the climb is gradual. Rest often and drink plenty of water. Do not depend on the waterholes along the trail as they may be frozen.

As on the first day, *ahu* mark the route. Across old lava flows the footpath is well worn and even sunken in spots. On the 1975 and 1984 flows, hikers have not had enough time to develop a distinct trail. The route goes from *ahu* to *ahu*, often across humpy, brittle lava. Watch your footing on the new flows.

Unlike the first day, the trail passes a series of cones and craters by which you can mark your progress. The first is Pukauahi (smoke hole), a red-brown prehistoric spatter cone, surrounded by 1984 lava. Next in line is Dewey Cone, named after the admiral who led the U.S. fleet in the Battle of Manila. The cone was formed by an eruption starting on July 4, 1899, shortly after the battle. You can easily recognize Dewey Cone from a distance by its symmetrical shape.

A little over a mile after Dewey comes Steaming Cone, built by the 1855 eruption. The cone no longer steams, but its red, orange, and green hue is a welcome change from the surrounding black, gray, and mustard-colored lava.

About two miles past Steaming Cone lies Pōhaku Hanalei, a tall, colorful, prehistoric spatter cone. A fissure from the 1984 eruption cut the cone and surrounded it with new lava. If it's late in the day, you can bivouac behind a rock windbreak near the cone. There is no water, however.

The two-mile stretch from Pōhaku Hanalei to the summit crater seems endless. Your legs and brain are working in slow motion. There are no distinct features, and the climbing is somewhat steeper.

Eventually, the North Pit and Moku'āweoweo, the summit caldera, heave in sight. Take a well-earned break and enjoy the eerie view. If it's getting late, nearby Jaggar's Cave makes an excellent bivouac. The cave is actually an open pit, but it is sheltered from the wind and does have a water hole next door. Thomas Jaggar, pioneering volcanologist and founder of the Hawaiian Volcano Observatory, used the cave on his field trips to study the mountain.

From Jaggar's Cave, the Mauna Loa Cabin is still a long, hard 2.1 miles away. The original cabin, built in 1934, stood near the cave. Don't you wish it were still there? In 1940 the cabin was moved to its present safer location farther along the crater rim. A lava flow from a summit eruption covered the original cement platform in 1984.

On the route to the present cabin are two craters, North Pit and Lua Poholo (pit that sank out of sight). North Pit is shallow, wide, and covered with smooth 1984 lava. Lua Poholo is a deep crater formed by a collapse in 1880. A huge ridge lies athwart its floor. Lava from the 1975 and 1984 eruptions has poured into the crater.

After 11.6 miles of walking, the Mauna Loa Cabin is a welcome sight.

It has 12 bunks with mattresses, a table, chairs, and a separate cooking area. Outside near the crater rim is a pit toilet. In back of the cabin is a water tank fed by rainfall collected on the roof. The water comes out distinctly brown so most people prefer a nearby water hole. To get to it from the cabin, walk south paralleling the crater rim on a well-worn path for about five minutes. Look for two *ahu* on a small rise to the left. They mark the waterhole in a deep crack. You can see the two *ahu* on the skyline from the kitchen window. Boil, filter, or chemically treat the water, whether from the tank or the crack.

On the way to the waterhole you pass by some rock windbreaks. Most are of twentieth century construction, but a few date from the Wilkes Expedition. His party of 50 spent almost a month in 1840 mapping the summit region. In the cleared area behind the present cabin is the site of a portable house that Wilkes used.

The view of the summit crater from the cabin (and the toilet!) is breathtaking. Moku'āweoweo (red fish section) is 2.7 miles long, 1.6 miles wide, and 600 feet deep in places. Steam still seeps from a fissure that opened the length of the crater in 1984. Lava from that eruption covers much of the floor. The tall cone in the center of the crater was built in 1940. Along the far rim and slightly to the left is the 1949 cone, colored red and green. The true summit, at 13,679 feet, is also along the far rim and slightly to the right. On the far left a gap in the crater wall leads to South Pit. North Pit is through a gap in the rim on the far right.

Route Description

From the Pu'u 'Ula'ula Rest House continue up the Mauna Loa Trail.

Climb gradually through prehistoric *pāhoehoe* and *'a'ā* lava flows.

Pass a line of red vents from the 1880 eruption.

Parallel a massive dark *'a'ā* flow on the left.

Go around to the left of a brown prehistoric spatter cone (map point 1). Look back for a last view of Pu'u 'Ula'ula.

Jog right and then left on smooth *pāhoehoe*.

On the left pass a series of multicolored spatter cones from the 1800 eruption. One has a pillar of lava.

Cross a narrow *'a'ā* flow from the 1899 eruption.

Climb steadily on 1855 *pāhoehoe* colored mustard brown. On the left, away from the trail, is a distinctive cone with a red notch.

On the right pass a line of spatter cones from the 1855 eruption. A short side trail leads to two deep red-orange vents.

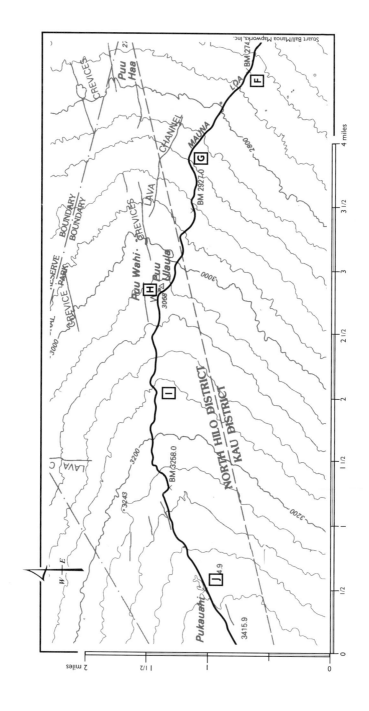

Bear left away from the cones on 1899 *pāhoehoe*.

Cross a 1984 flow of new *pāhoehoe* lava. Keep track of the *ahu* as the treadway is indistinct in spots.

Reach the base of Pukauahi, a brownish prehistoric spatter cone (map point J).

Turn left and skirt the base of the cone on a path of pumice.

Negotiate very brittle *pāhoehoe* from the 1984 eruption.

Switch to smooth prehistoric *pāhoehoe*. The grooved trail makes for easy walking.

On the right, well off the trail, is a line of red cones with white sulphur deposits.

Reach a pole with a sign marking Dewey Cone (map point K). It's the large dark cone in back, built by the eruption of 1899.

The trail splits. Keep right. (The left fork is the old trail which was covered by a 1984 flow.)

Go around a low red cone of prehistoric origin. Lava flows from 1984 are to the left and right.

Cross mustard-colored *pāhoehoe* from the 1855 eruption.

Follow a deep trench on the right. It carried lava downslope from Steaming Cone in 1855.

Descend into the trench and climb out of it.

Jog right and then left on 1855 *'a'ā*.

Climb steadily past Steaming Cone on old gray *pāhoehoe*. Olive-green pumice partially covers the lava.

Pass a pole with a sign marking Steaming Cone (map point L).

The black *'a'ā* flow on the left is from the 1855 eruption.

Reach a sign marking a water hole. It's just off the trail to the left in a collapsed lava tube.

Traverse a long stretch of jumbled-up *pāhoehoe*.

Reach the 12,000-foot elevation marker (map point M).

Cross shattered *pāhoehoe* from the 1975 and 1984 eruptions.

Follow a line of 1975 spatter cones toward Pōhaku Hanalei, the tall prehistoric cone upslope.

Parallel a channel filled with 1984 lava from a recent vent inside the cone.

Pass a rock windbreak and bivouac on the right.

Hug the base of Pōhaku Hanalei to avoid walking on the 1984 flow (map point N). Huge chunks of red-orange lava line the trail.

Behind Pōhaku Hanalei work left and then right, following a line of spatter cones from the 1984 eruption.

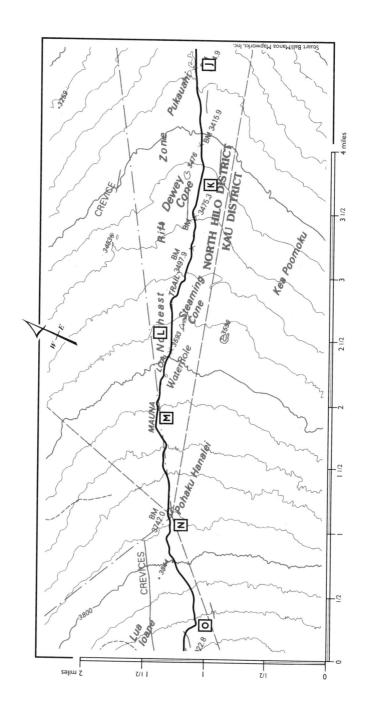

Angle left away from the cones across shiny 1984 *pāhoehoe*.

Climb more steeply on old rough *pāhoehoe*. Take it easy on this section! Look back at the line of cones you've passed. On the horizon is the notched one just above Pu'u 'Ula'ula.

Bear right, through the 1935 *'a'ā* flow (map point O) and then continue straight up.

Reach an unsigned junction. Turn right, across the slope. (The abandoned trail to the left is an old route to the cabin.)

Turn left upslope on 1984 *pāhoehoe* lava.

Cross fissures from the 1975 and 1984 eruptions.

Return to old lava covered with pumice.

North Pit and Moku'āweoweo, the summit crater, come into view.

Shortly afterward, reach a junction and the 13,000-foot elevation marker (map point P). Turn left and down into North Pit on the Cabin Trail. (The trail to the right leads to Jaggar's Cave, a water hole, and the Summit and Observatory Trails.)

Cross North Pit on smooth *pāhoehoe* from the 1984 summit eruption. The summit cabin is visible in the distance along the left rim of Moku'āweoweo Crater.

At the far side of North Pit the lava becomes mounded and broken up.

Skirt to the right of a deep pit crater, known as Lua Poholo (map point Q). Don't get too close to the rim as it's riddled with cracks.

Climb gradually up to the rim of the main crater.

Negotiate a seemingly long, extremely rough section on prehistoric flows. (This is the stretch that everyone curses in the cabin logbooks.)

Pass a trail sign on the left. Keep right, along the rim.

At the top of the next rise, the cabin roof comes into view.

Pass a monumental *ahu* on the rim to the right.

Almost immediately, reach the Mauna Loa Cabin (elev. 13,250 ft) (map point R).

DAY FOUR—Layover at Mauna Loa Cabin

If the symptoms of altitude sickness return, take it easy today or even head back down to Pu'u 'Ula'ula. If you are feeling fine, there are several superb side trips. To get to the actual summit, retrace your steps to Jaggar's Cave and pick up the Summit Trail there. Round-trip distance is 9.2 miles.

To cross the crater, descend a very steep landslide from the rim near the cabin water hole. Keep the 1940 cone on your right and climb out of the crater on the 1949 cone. Turn right, along the rim, to reach the true summit. Return via the Summit and Cabin Trails.

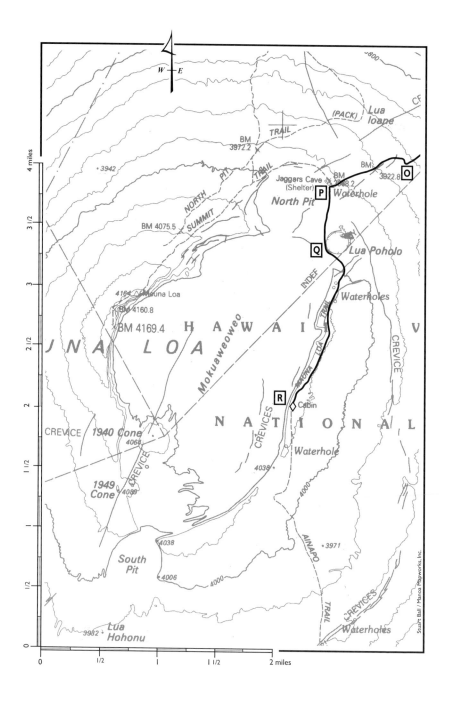

A complete circumnavigation of the crater rim is also possible. Start clockwise from the cabin so you hike the difficult cross-country section first. The *pāhoehoe* lava around South Pit is very weak and may collapse when walked on. Wear long pants to avoid bloody legs.

Another option is to hike part way down the ʻĀinapō Trail, a route to the summit crater used originally by early Hawaiians. The trail starts near the cabin water hole and is marked by small *ahu* and blotches of yellow paint on the lava. Remember, in this case, what goes down must come up.

At an altitude of 13,000 feet none of the hikes mentioned above is a trivial exercise. Take a map, first aid kit, food, water, and extra clothing in your day pack. Turn back if heavy clouds start to build up near the crater.

After dinner, watch the sun set and the stars come out. The clear air and dark sky make this spot one of the best in the world for star gazing. It also must be one of the quietest spots on earth. When the wind dies down, there is no sound whatsoever.

DAY FIVE—Mauna Loa Cabin to Puʻu ʻUlaʻula

Length: 11.6 mi

Elev. Loss: 3,200 ft

Today, retrace your steps along the Cabin Trail to North Pit and then down the Mauna Loa Trail to Puʻu ʻUlaʻula Rest House. The walking is exceedingly pleasant. Just put one foot in front of the other and let gravity carry you down the mountain.

Do all the things you didn't feel like doing on the way up. Take pictures. Explore some of the cones and pits. Figure out which lava flow you're hiking on. Enjoy the expansive views as the mountain unfolds before you.

DAY SIX—Puʻu ʻUlaʻula to Mauna Loa lookout

Length: 7.5 mi

Elev. Loss: 3,400 ft

Today, descend to the trailhead at the Mauna Loa lookout. Like yesterday, the walking is easy, leaving plenty of time for sightseeing.

Stop at the lone ʻōhiʻa tree just above the 8,000-foot marker. Stretch out on the lava and enjoy the warm sun. Take in the returning greenery below you and then, reluctantly, head down to civilization.

Options

This trip has several variations, most involving the time spent on the mountain. The minimum stay is three days, two up and one down. To reach the true summit, you need four days. If you experience altitude sickness, you should take at least five days. The trip as described is a leisurely six days, two up and two down with two layover days.

The Observatory Trail is an optional route to and from the summit crater. The trail starts from the Mauna Loa Observatory at 11,055 feet and ends near Jaggar's Cave. Total distance is 3.8 miles, and the elevation gain/loss is about 2,000 feet. Its short length makes the Observatory Trail quite attractive as a route down the mountain. Unfortunately, you need to have a second car parked at the Observatory, which involves a complicated 125-mile shuttle from Hilo. Use the trail as an exit only if you can arrange to have someone pick you up.

The Observatory Trail is also very seductive as a route up Mauna Loa. Try it as part of a day hike to the actual summit, perhaps, but not as an overnight trip. You are asking too much of your body to climb six miles to the summit cabin and adjust to 13,250 feet of elevation in one day. Your first night at the cabin could be the most miserable one in your life.

Another route up or down Mauna Loa is the 'Āinapō Trail. It starts from Route 11 past Volcano village between mile markers 40 and 41. The first eight miles are along a dirt road through ranch land and then native 'ōhi'a-koa forest. At 10.7 miles and 7,750 feet elevation is a small, but luxurious, cabin maintained by the Hawai'i Division of Forestry. Phone them at (808) 933–4221 for a camping permit and more information. Past the cabin, the 'Āinapō Trail climbs 5,500 feet in about 7.5 miles to the summit cabin. The route is marked by small *ahu* and blotches of yellow paint on the lava.

If you don't have the time or energy to climb Mauna Loa, try the Nāpau Crater trip. It's shorter and at lower elevation than Mauna Loa, and you see similar volcanic features.

4. NĀPAU CRATER

Type:	Mountain
Length:	2–3 days, 12.2 mi
Elev. Loss:	1,200 ft
Difficulty:	Low
Location:	Hawai'i (the Big Island): Hawai'i Volcanoes National Park
Topo Map:	Makaopuhi Crater, Volcano, Kalalua

Highlights

This trip takes you across barren lava flows and through lush green rain forest. The route leads to Pu'u 'Ō'ō, a recently active vent of Kīlauea Volcano. Along the way you see volcanic shields, pit craters, spatter cones, and tree molds. The only negative is that the campsite at Nāpau Crater has no water.

Planning

Call or write the National Park for a brochure, trail map, and camping information. The visitor center phone number is (808) 967–7311, and the address is Superintendent, Hawai'i Volcanoes National Park, HI 96718.

Bring a tent and a light sleeping bag as there is no shelter at the campsite. It does rain there, usually at night or in the early morning and especially during winter. At an elevation of 2,720 feet the campsite can be chilly at night, even in summer.

If possible, plan to arrive on the Big Island at Hilo. The driving instructions below start from the Hilo Airport. All major rental car firms have booths there.

There is a public bus, known as Hele-on, from Hilo to the National Park once a day. Call the Hawai'i County Transit System at (808) 935–8241 for the current schedule.

If you are arriving at Keāhole Airport near Kailua (Kona), you have a longer drive. Exit Keāhole Airport and turn right on Queen Ka'ahumanu Hwy (Rte 19) to Kailua (Kona). There, pick up Hawai'i Belt Rd. (Rte 11) and follow it around the southern tip of the island to the National Park. The distance to the trailhead is 112 miles and the driving time, about 2¼ hours.

Coleman fuel (white gas) is available at the 7-Eleven stores in Hilo,

Hirano Store in Glenwood, and Volcano Store in Volcano. All three have some food items. For a wider selection stop at Safeway in the Prince Kūhiō Plaza or KTA Super Stores. Both are along Kanoelehua Ave. on the way out of Hilo.

Once in the park stop at the Kīlauea Visitor Center to get a back-country permit. The center is open from 7:30 A.M. to 4:45 P.M. seven days a week. Fill your water bottles and bags there as water is not available at the trailhead. Take a minimum of 2.5 gallons per person for the three-day trip. I know water is heavy, but you only have to lug all of it in the first day.

Trailhead Directions

Distance: (Hilo Airport to Mauna Ulu trailhead)—37 mi

Driving Time: 1 hr

Exit Hilo Airport on Airport Rd.

At the first traffic light, turn left on Kanoelehua Ave. (Rte 11) to Volcano.

Kanoelehua Ave. becomes Hawai'i Belt Rd. (still Rte 11).

Just past Kea'au, the road narrows to two lanes.

Ascend gradually, passing the villages of Kurtistown, Mountain View, and Glenwood.

Pass turnoffs to Volcano village on the right.

Enter Hawai'i Volcanoes National Park.

Shortly afterward, turn left at the sign for the park entrance.

Pay the fee at the entrance station.

Stop at Kīlauea Visitor Center on the right (elev. 3,974 ft). There, get a backcountry permit for Nāpau Crater and ask about current trail conditions. Remember to fill your water bottles.

Drive back toward the entrance station.

Just before reaching it, turn right on Crater Rim Dr.

Turn left at the stop sign.

Pass Kīlauea Iki overlook on the right and Thurston (Nāhuku) lava tube on the left.

Wind through a tree fern and 'ōhi'a forest.

Pass the turnoff to Pu'u Pua'i on the right.

At the next intersection turn left on Chain of Craters Rd.

On the right pass the turnoff to Hilina Pali overlook.

Just past Pauahi Crater turn left into Mauna Ulu parking area (elev. 3,220 ft) (map point A). If you have only one car, leave it there and start hiking. If you have two cars, drop off people and packs, as necessary, and continue down Chain of Craters Rd. in both cars.

After passing Muliwai a Pele turnout, look for Kealakomo overlook and picnic area (elev. 2,000 ft) (map point N). It is marked by a wooden pavilion on the right. Park one car there.

In the other car backtrack up Chain of Craters Rd. Turn right into Mauna Ulu parking area and leave the car there.

DAY ONE—Mauna Ulu to Nāpau Crater

Length: 7 mi

Elev. Loss: 500 ft

On the first day the route descends gradually along the upper East Rift Zone of Kīlauea Volcano. The zone is an area of structural weakness, here marked by a line of spatter cones, volcanic shields, and pit craters. Lava from recent eruptions has engulfed huge patches of the rain forest growing on older flows.

About a mile in, climb Pu'u Huluhulu (shaggy hill) for a view of the ravaged landscape. The hill is actually a spatter cone that formed 300 to 400 years ago. Next to it to the north is a small forested crater. Recent lava flows have almost completely surrounded both the cone and the crater.

Nearby to the south is Mauna Ulu (growing mountain), a volcanic shield created by an eruption lasting from 1969 to 1974. Lava poured out of several vents that later merged to form a lava lake at the summit. Some of the flows crossed the old Chain of Craters Rd., plunged spectacularly over Hōlei Pali, and entered the ocean.

Next in line down the rift zone is Makaopuhi (eye of the eel), which used to be a double crater. In 1973 a lava flow from Mauna Ulu filled the deep western pit and partially covered the eastern pit. The forested hill to the north is Kāne Nui o Hamo, a volcanic shield formed about 600 years ago.

Extending from the rim of Makaopuhi Crater is the lush native rain forest. It is dominated here by hapu'u tree ferns and 'ōhi'a lehua trees. 'Ōhi'a colonizes recent lava flows and reaches maturity on older flows, such as this one. The delicate red flowers grow in clusters. Native birds, such as 'apapane and 'i'iwi, feed on the nectar and help in pollination.

With their sweeping fronds the hapu'u tree ferns form a nearly continuous understory in the native forest here. Their trunks consist of roots tightly woven around a small central stem. The brown fiber covering the young fronds of hapu'u is called *pulu*. From about 1860 to 1885 pulu was harvested nearby to become pillow and mattress stuffing. A factory processed the fiber and shipped it to California from Keauhou landing (see the Halapē trip). The remains of the factory are just off the trail before the campsite.

After setting up camp, take a short walk to Nāpau (the endings) Crater overlook. The view of the crater and Pu'u 'Ō'ō beyond is eerie, especially in the evening or on a moonlit night. If the vent is still active, you will be treated to the greatest show on earth.

Route Description

At the far end of the parking area walk past a barrier across the road.

Shortly afterward, turn left off the road on to the Nāpau Trail. On the right is a kiosk, displaying trail maps and information.

Cross the lava flow of 1973. The trail is marked by piles of rocks, called *ahu*. They are known as cairns on the mainland.

Enter a remnant 'ōhi'a forest and then pass some tree molds.

Bear right toward Pu'u Huluhulu, a forested cone. The ropy *pāhoehoe* lava underfoot was formed during the 1974 eruption of Mauna Ulu.

Reach a junction at the base of Pu'u Huluhulu (map point B). Drop your pack and take the short side trail to the top of the cone (elev. 3,440 ft). From there you can see much of the East Rift Zone of Kīlauea Volcano. Close up to the south is Mauna Ulu, a volcanic shield with a lava lake. To the east lies the route of this trip past Makaopuhi Crater to the Pu'u 'Ō'ō cone. Mauna Loa is the massive mountain in the distance to the west.

Resume hiking on the main trail. Initially, it hugs the base of Pu'u Huluhulu.

Descend gradually and then swing right, around Mauna Ulu.

Climb to a small pit crater (map point C).

Bear left and pass some steam vents.

Descend gradually toward Makaopuhi Crater on the 1973 lava flow. The hill to the left of the crater is Kāne Nui o Hamo, an old volcanic shield similar to Mauna Ulu.

Reach the crater rim (map point D) and turn right along it.

Enter the lush green rain forest.

Reach the junction with the Kalapana Trail (map point E). Continue straight, along the crater rim. (To the right the Kalapana Trail leads down to Chain of Craters Rd. and is the return route of this trip.)

Cross the tip of the 1968–1969 flows several times (map point F). The lava there is the 'a'ā type—rough, clinkery, and hard to walk on.

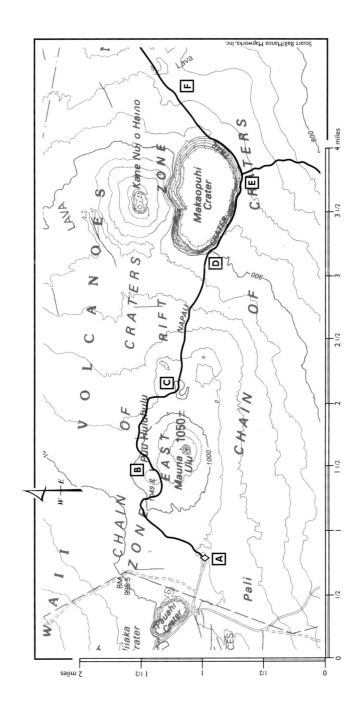

Stuart Ball/Manoa Mapworks, Inc.

Pass a pulu factory.

Reach a junction (map point G). Take the left fork to the campsite. (The right fork leads to an overlook of Nāpau Crater.)

Descend briefly to the camping area (elev. 2,720 ft) (map point H). There are several good tent sites on both sides of the main trail. A short side trail leads to a pit toilet.

DAY TWO—Day hike toward Pu'u 'Ō'ō

Length: 7 mi round trip

Elev. Gain/Loss: 400/400 ft

The day hike leads to an area in the middle East Rift Zone that has experienced intermittent volcanic activity since 1983. In January of that year the eruption began with a line of fountains along a fissure. Activity concentrated at the Pu'u 'Ō'ō vent, which gradually formed a spatter cone and a lava lake. Flows from the eruption eventually entered the sea, after destroying houses in the Royal Gardens subdivision, and the Waha'ula Visitor Center and Kamoamoa campground in the National Park.

One of the flows has created a forest of tree molds near the cone. The molds form when *pāhoehoe* lava surrounds the trunk of an 'ōhi'a tree and solidifies against it. The lava then drains downslope, leaving a shell of cooled lava around the tree. The tree burns, resulting in a hollow pillar.

Before you start hiking today, three cautions are in order. First, the day hike follows an unmaintained trail that is rough and poorly marked. The Park Service neither encourages nor discourages its use. Try it only if you are an experienced hiker with good route-finding skills.

Second, wear long pants. When walked on, the new *pāhoehoe* lava near the cone may collapse, leaving a hole with jagged edges. Bare legs get bloody very quickly.

Third, keep your distance from any active lava flows. The heat is a natural deterrent, but be aware of your position at all times. Stay upwind from the flow to avoid suffocating gases. Stay upslope because lava can move and spread rapidly.

Route Description

Continue along the trail past the last tent site.

Shortly afterward, reach the edge of a lava flow. Turn right, down the flow, following the *ahu*.

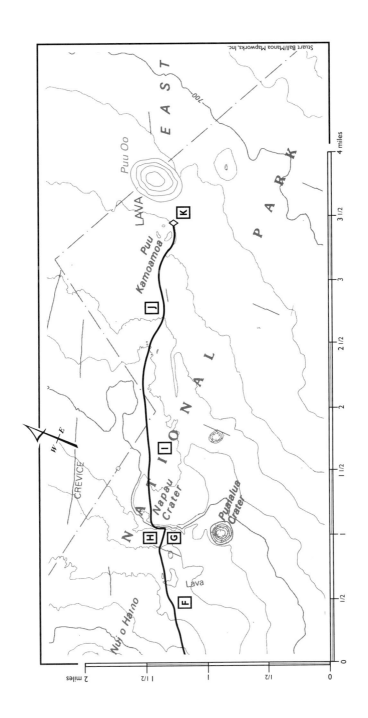

Pass some tree molds.

Turn left across the flow by the rim of Nāpau Crater.

Turn right and descend steeply into the crater over an ʻaʻā flow.

Cross the crater on an indistinct trail marked by small *ahu*. The floor is covered by the lava flows of 1968 and 1983.

Climb out of the crater between two small cones (map point I).

Keep to the left of a large crack.

Proceed along the 1968 flow.

Cross a small crack filled with ʻōhiʻa and tree fern.

The flow narrows.

Climb over two rises.

Reach a junction (map point J). Take the right fork. (The left fork also leads to Puʻu ʻŌʻō.)

Keep to the right of a line of ramparts.

Go through an area of broken, twisted lava.

Climb briefly and then descend gradually toward Puʻu ʻŌʻō.

The trail peters out (map point K). On the left are some tree molds in a field of pumice. On the right is a line of fumaroles, vents with heavy sulphur deposits.

Approach Puʻu ʻŌʻō cone, vent, lava lake, and flows cautiously. Remember to stay well clear of any signs of activity.

After exploring the area, return to the campsite via the same route.

DAY THREE—Nāpau Crater to Kealakomo overlook

Length: 5.2 mi

Elev. Loss: 700 ft

The route today is mostly downhill, first through lush fern forest and then across barren lava flows from Mauna Ulu. In the early seventies those flows repeatedly cut the old Chain of Craters Rd., resulting in its abandonment. Short sections of the road are still visible.

Watch closely for the square orange markers through the forest as the trail is occasionally indistinct there.

Route Description

Backtrack to the junction with the Kalapana Trail (map point E). Turn left down it.

Descend gradually through native forest dominated by tree fern. The trail is marked by orange squares tacked to the trees.

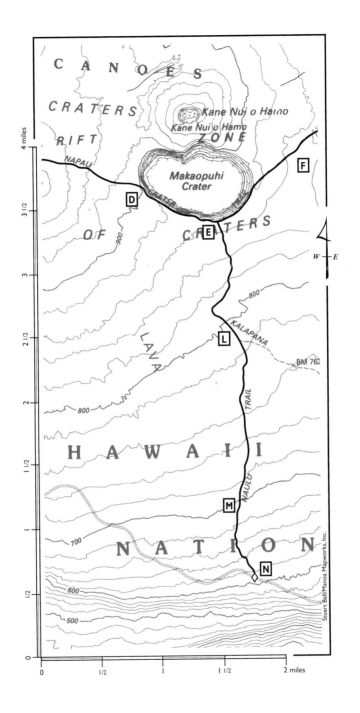

Break out into the open suddenly and cross a barren 'a'ā lava flow. The route is marked by *ahu*.

The lava becomes smooth *pāhoehoe*. The flow originated from Mauna Ulu in 1972.

Reach an exposed section of the old Chain of Craters Rd.

Cross another patch of the old road.

Shortly afterward, reach the junction with the Nāulu Trail (map point L). Bear right on it. (To the left the Kalapana Trail continues down to the coast at Lae'apuki; however, a lava flow has recently blocked the trail at its intersection with Chain of Craters Rd.)

Cross another section of pavement, and then the road disappears for good under the lava.

The flow underfoot is now from the 1971 eruption of Mauna Ulu.

Parallel a narrow band of grass and scattered 'ōhi'a trees. Bear right and cross it (map point M).

Bear left and descend next to the band of trees.

Cross a short stretch of 'a'ā and then return to *pāhoehoe*.

Bear left into the band of 'ōhi'a.

Descend briefly on an old 'a'ā flow.

Reach Chain of Craters Rd. at Kealakomo overlook (elev. 2,000 ft) (map point N).

Options

There are several variations of this trip, none as attractive as the route described. You can, of course, do the trip in reverse. It's all uphill, making for a good workout with all that water in your pack!

Groups with limited time can make a two-day trip. Hike to the campsite the first day. Take the day hike in the morning and exit in the afternoon of the second day.

Parties with only one car can return via the same route to the Mauna Ulu trailhead or do the trip as described and hitchhike back up Chain of Craters Rd.

5. Waimanu Valley

Type:	Shoreline
Length:	2–3 days, 18.0 mi round trip
Elev. Gain/Loss:	3,600/3,600 ft
Difficulty:	Medium
Location:	Hawai'i (the Big Island): Kohala Forest Reserve, Waimanu National Estuarine Research Reserve
Topo Map:	Kukuihaele, Honokāne

Highlights

This trip traverses an isolated section of the rugged Kohala coast. Sheer sea cliffs alternate with deep, lush windward valleys. Along the way are black sand beaches, myriad streams and gulches, cool swimming holes and roaring waterfalls.

Planning

Call or write the Hawai'i Division of Forestry for a brochure, trail map, and camping permit information. The phone number is (808) 933–4221, and the address is P. O. Box 4849, Hilo, HI 96720. Office hours are 8 A.M. to 4 P.M., Monday through Friday.

Forestry currently issues permits no earlier than one month in advance of your trip. The permit assigns you to one of 10 numbered campsites in Waimanu Valley. Sites 2 through 7 are all good. Campsite 3 is very spacious if you have a large group.

Summer (May–October) is the best time of year to take this trip. The weather is usually drier then, and the streams are easier to cross. Whenever you go, be prepared for rain and high water.

Bring a good tent and put all your dry gear in plastic bags. Pack a light sleeping bag or liner because the nights can be chilly, especially in winter. Take repellant as the mosquitoes are fierce along the middle section of the route. The campsites are relatively free of the pests because of the trade winds. *Tabis* (Japanese reef walkers) with their fuzzy bottoms are perfect for exploring the slippery, rocky shoreline.

If possible, plan to arrive on the Big Island at Hilo. The driving instructions below start from the Hilo Airport. All major rental car firms have booths there.

If you arrive at Keāhole Airport near Kailua (Kona), you have a slightly longer drive. Exit Keāhole Airport and turn left on Queen Ka'ahumanu Hwy (Rte 19) toward Kawaihae. Just before there, turn right on Kawaihae Rd. (still Rte 19) to Waimea. There turn left on Hawai'i Belt Rd. (still Rte 19) to Honoka'a. There turn left on Rte 240 and follow the regular instructions below to Waipi'o lookout. The distance to the trailhead is 58 miles, and the driving time, about 1½ hours.

Coleman fuel (white gas) is available at 7-Eleven stores and supermarkets in Hilo. The trailhead, Waipi'o lookout, has covered picnic tables, restrooms, and a water fountain where you can fill your water bottles.

Waipi'o lookout, however, is not a safe place to park your car overnight. Instead, leave it at Waipi'o Artworks, which is a 15-minute walk from the trailhead. The directions are given below. Call the Artworks at (808) 775-0958 to find out the current fee and let them know when you're coming.

Trailhead Directions

Distance: (Hilo Airport to Waipi'o lookout)—52 mi

Driving Time: 1¼ hr

Exit Hilo Airport on Airport Rd.
At the first traffic light, turn right on Kanoelehua Ave. (Rte 11).
At the road end, turn left on Kamehameha Hwy.
The road forks; keep right on Bayfront Hwy around Hilo Bay.
Bayfront Hwy becomes Hawai'i Belt Rd. (Rte 19).
Proceed along the Hāmākua Coast past a series of villages.
Drive through Laupāhoehoe village.
Cross Laupāhoehoe and Ka'awali'i Gulches.
Turn right on Route 240 to Honoka'a.
Drive through Honoka'a town.
The road jogs right and then left.
Shortly afterward, reach Waipi'o lookout (elev. 904 ft) (map point A). Drop off people and packs, as necessary.
Drive back to where the road jogs, this time to the right. Turn left and down on a paved road.
Cross a one-lane bridge.
Reach Kukuihaele village.

Look for Waipi'o Artworks on the left. Park in the lot across the street from the Artworks. Pay the overnight parking fee at the Artworks and walk back to the lookout.

DAY ONE—Waipi'o lookout to Waimanu Valley

Length: 9 mi

Elev. Gain/Loss: 1,350/2,250 ft

Start early today as the hike is a long nine miles with plenty of elevation change. Initially, the route descends steeply into Waipi'o Valley on a paved road. After crossing Wailoa Stream, you pick up the Waimanu Trail. It ascends steeply out of Waipi'o Valley and winds through 13 gulches. The route finishes with another steep descent, into Waimanu Valley, and a stream crossing to the campsites.

Before starting, enjoy the marvelous view from Waipi'o lookout. The valley lies about 1,000 feet below and extends deep into the Kohala Mountains. A series of waterfalls cascade down the far wall. You can make out the Waimanu Trail as it zigzags up the cliffs near the ocean.

In ancient times Waipi'o (curved water) Valley was one of the major population centers on the Big Island. The fertile valley supported a thriving community based on taro farming and fish raising. Waipi'o Valley was said to be a favorite haunt of Hawaiian royalty. Today only a few taro farmers remain.

In Waipi'o Valley you must cross wide Wailoa Stream. The route narrative describes the best places to ford. Do not attempt to cross if the stream is obviously swollen from heavy rain in the back of the valley. The same warning applies to the stream in Waimanu Valley.

Like most trails, the Waimanu has both good and bad sections. While contouring through the gulches, the trail is wide and graded. It makes a pleasant stroll except for the cloud of mosquitoes that usually follows you. On the switchbacks, the trail is often rough and narrow. Watch your footing constantly, especially on the steep descent into Waimanu Valley.

Much of lower Waimanu (bird water) Valley is an estuary and wetland. It is home to native species of 'o'opu (goby), hīhīwai (mollusk), and 'opae (shrimp). The fresh water comes from elevated springs and five waterfalls that plunge over the western wall of the valley.

In the 1800s several hundred people lived in Waimanu Valley. They grew taro and fruits and raised fish in ponds. The last inhabitants left the valley in 1946 after a destructive tsunami (sea wave). Waimanu Valley contains many archeological sites, including rock enclosures, terraces, taro ponds, irrigation systems, and *heiau* (religious sites).

The campsites in Waimanu Valley are strung out along the beach in a grove of ironwood trees. Nearby are two elevated compost toilets. The water source is Waimanu Stream or Keawewai, a small stream from an elevated spring near the far end of the beach. To get there, see the directions for tomorrow's day hike. As always, boil, filter, or chemically treat the water.

Route Description:

Take the one-lane paved road leading into Waipi'o Valley.

Initially, the road switches back twice and crosses a narrow, fast flowing stream.

Descend very steeply down the side of the valley. Watch out for four-wheel drive vehicles.

At the bottom reach a junction (map point B). Take a sharp right toward the beach. (The road to the left heads farther into the valley.)

The road becomes dirt and then sand.

Before reaching the shore, enter a grove of ironwood trees.

The road curves left and parallels the black sand beach.

Reach Wailoa (long water) Stream and ford it (map point C). There is no official crossing. The stream is narrower and shallower at its mouth near the ocean; however, the current there can be very strong. As an alternative, ford the stream to the left at its widest point. The current is less noticeable there, but the water is waist deep. Do not cross the stream between its mouth and widest point unless you enjoy swimming with your pack!

On the opposite bank pick up a wide path paralleling the beach.

Stroll through stands of ironwood. The low-lying shrub near the shore is naupaka kahakai.

At the far end of the beach pass some standing water on the left.

Just after the water, turn left into the forest along the edge of the valley floor.

On the left pass a small plot surrounded by barbed wire.

Almost immediately reach a junction marked by a hand-painted sign (map point D). Keep right on the Waimanu Trail, which is the less traveled route uphill. (The trail to the left leads into Waipi'o Valley.)

Climb the valley wall on seven long switchbacks.

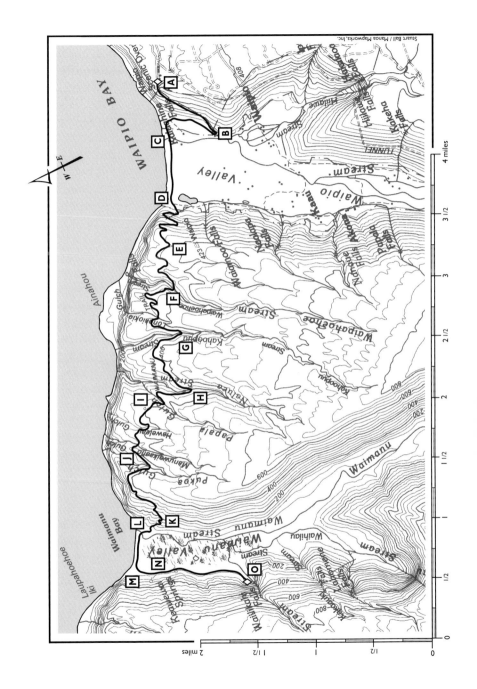

Stuart Ball / Manoa Mapworks, Inc.

At the fourth is a superb view point. The beach and ocean are directly below. You can see well into Waipi'o Valley. The waterfall along the coast is Kaluahine (the old lady).

After the fifth switchback go through an ironwood grove. The upper switchbacks are less steep and more shady than the lower ones.

After the seventh switchback reach the top of the ridge. Turn left through a small clearing in the ironwoods.

Work into and out of a dry gulch with huge albizia, eucalyptus, and evergreen trees (map point E).

Descend into a second gulch and cross a stream. Climb out through ironwoods.

Descend into a deep ravine.

Pass a small waterfall with a deep pool. Time for a quick dip?

Cross Waipāhoehoe (smooth lava water) Stream (map point F).

Climb out of the ravine on three switchbacks through hala and ironwood trees.

Work into and out of two small gulches known as Kalaniwahine and Lonokiokio.

Descend into a wide ravine.

Cross Kaho'opu'u (the heaped up) Stream above a small, but inviting pool (map point G).

Climb out of the ravine and traverse a broad side-ridge.

Cross a small, dry gulch.

Descend into another wide ravine.

Cross Naluea (nausea) Stream (map point H) and climb out of the ravine.

Work into and out of Pāpala Gulch.

Cross a wide side-ridge.

Reach a rundown shelter with two-seater pit toilets (map point I).

Work into and out of a dry gulch.

Descend into and climb out of Haweleau Gulch.

Descend into and climb out of Manuwaika'alio Gulch, which has a double stream.

On the next side-ridge reach the high point on the trail (elev. 1,360 ft) (map point J).

Work into and out of Pūkoa Gulch.

Cross over the next side-ridge. You can now see the ocean and hear the surf of Waimanu Bay. The two peninsulas along the coast are Laupāhoehoeiki (small smooth lava flat) and Laupāhoehoenui (large smooth lava flat).

Descend steadily into Waimanu Valley on seven switchbacks (map point K). Watch your footing on the loose rock. The trail is narrow in spots because of landslides. Look for Wai'ilikahi Falls across the valley.

Descend steeply on a series of S-shaped curves.

Reach the valley floor and turn right, toward the ocean.

Pass a camping sign on the left.

Emerge into an open, grassy area.

Pass an elevated compost toilet on the right.

Reach Waimanu Stream and ford it (map point L). Again, there is no official crossing. Like Wailoa, Waimanu Stream is narrower and shallower at its mouth near the ocean; however, the current can be stronger there. A bit inland the stream is more wide, deep, and slow moving. Take your pick.

Once across, find your assigned campsite.

DAY TWO—Day hike to Wai'ilikahi Falls

Length: 3 mi

Elev. Gain/Loss: 200/200 ft

If you wish, take the half-day hike to Wai'ilikahi Falls. The trail there is muddy and obscure in spots and mosquito-ridden. Look for surveyors ribbon left by previous groups. The falls and limpid pool below are extraordinarily beautiful and well worth the walk. Wai'ilikahi means water with a single surface.

On the way to the falls you pass through groves of mountain apple. The trees have large, oblong, shiny leaves. In spring the purple flowers carpet the trail. The delicious pink or red fruit usually ripens in late July or early August. Just shake the tree and try to catch the apples as they come down. The species is native to Malaysia and was brought over by the early Hawaiians.

There are lots of other possibilities for today. Sunbathe on the black sand beach. Explore along the coast to Laupāhoehoeiki or Laupāhoehoenui. Go swimming in the ocean and then rinse off in Waimanu Stream. Keep in mind that Waimanu Bay is on the exposed windward coast of the Big Island. The sea and its currents are very powerful there. Never turn your back on the ocean.

Perhaps the most attractive activity, especially in the afternoon, is doing absolutely nothing. Find a comfortable spot and kick back. Take in the broad sweep of the bay and its towering sea cliffs. Watch the surf pound the black rocks and roll up the beach. Listen for the wind soughing through the ironwoods. This is the life.

Route Description:

From your campsite walk along the shore away from Waimanu Stream. The beach changes from rock to sand.

Just past the last campsite, turn left into the valley (map point M).

Keep a large pool of standing water on your left.

Push through a patch of ferns.

Pick up a makeshift trail as the ground vegetation thins under a canopy of kukui trees.

Cross a small stream known as Keawewai (map point N). It comes from a spring and waterfall in the side of the valley.

Cross a second stream, also from an elevated spring.

Continue walking along the edge of the valley floor through groves of mountain apple.

Negotiate a thick hau tangle.

Work right and begin climbing up a side ravine.

Wai'ilikahi Stream comes in on the left. Follow it upstream.

Reach Wai'ilikahi Falls (map point O). At its base is a good-sized swimming hole.

DAY THREE—Waimanu Valley to Waipi'o lookout

Length: 9 mi

Elev. Gain/Loss: 2,250/1,350 ft

Retrace your steps back to Waipi'o lookout. The return trip is more difficult because it includes two steep climbs and only one descent.

Options:

Variations of this trip are limited. No camping is allowed in Waipi'o Valley. The Waimanu Trail ends at Waimanu Valley so the route out is the same as the way in.

Groups with limited time can take only two days. Without the middle layover day, however, the trip just turns into a tough grind. Besides, you would miss seeing lovely Wai'ilikahi Falls.

Beach with palm trees at Halapē. Halapē trip. (Photo by Deborah Uchida)

Moonset over the Ka'ū Coast. Ka'aha trip. (Photo by Deborah Uchida)

Moonrise over Keauhou. Halapē trip. (Photo by Deborah Uchida)

Tide pool at Keauhou. Halapē trip. (Photo by Deborah Uchida)

Sea arch. Kaʻaha trip. (Photo by Deborah Uchida)

Pepeiao Cabin in sight. Kaʻaha trip. (Photo by Deborah Uchida)

Sunrise at Kaʻaha. Kaʻaha trip. (Photo by Deborah Uchida)

Starting for the Kaʻū Coast. Kaʻaha trip. (Photo by Deborah Uchida)

Crossing Waimanu Stream. Waimanu Valley trip. (Photo by Deborah Uchida)

Approaching Pōhaku Hanalei cone. Mauna Loa trip. (Photo by Deborah Uchida)

Waimanu Stream and Valley. Waimanu Valley trip. (Photo by Deborah Uchida)

Waimanu Bay. Waimanu Valley trip. (Photo by Deborah Uchida)

Waipiʻo Bay and Valley. Waimanu Valley trip. (Photo by Deborah Uchida)

KAUA'I

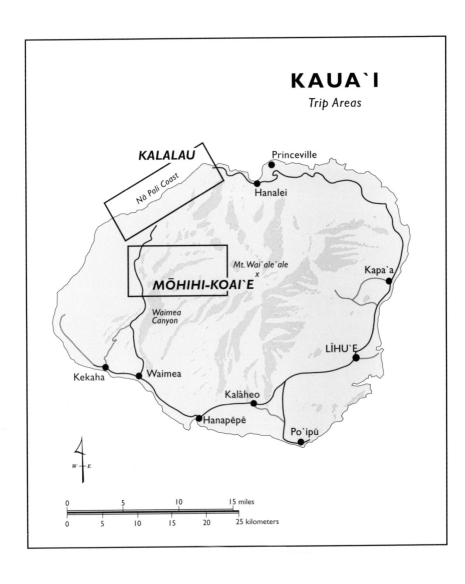

KAUA`I

Trip Areas

KALALAU

Princeville

Nā Pali Coast

Hanalei

Mt. Wai`ale`ale
x

Kapa`a

MŌHIHI-KOAI`E

Waimea Canyon

LĪHU`E

Kekaha Waimea

Kalāheo

Hanapēpē

Po`ipū

W ─ E

0	5	10	15 miles
0	5	10 15 20	25 kilometers

6. KALALAU

Type:	Shoreline
Length:	2–4 days, 22.0 mi round trip
Elev. Gain/Loss:	2,400/2,400 ft
Difficulty:	Medium
Location:	Kauaʻi: Nā Pali Coast State Park, Honoonāpali Natural Area Reserve
Topo Map:	Hāʻena

Highlights

Kalalau is the classic tourist backpacking trip in Hawaiʻi. The route winds along the rugged Nā Pali Coast past vertical sea cliffs and into deep, lush gulches. Along the way are rushing streams, cascading waterfalls, and the surging ocean below. At the end is a wide sandy beach backed by the towering, fluted walls of Kalalau Valley.

Planning

Call or write the Kauaʻi Division of State Parks for camping permit information. The phone number is (808) 241–3444, and the address is 3060 ʻEīwa St., Līhuʻe, HI 96766. You can also get a permit from the State Parks office in Honolulu. The phone number is (808) 587–0300, and the address is P. O. Box 621, Honolulu, HI 96809.

Pick up a copy of *On the Nā Pali Coast* by Kathy Valier. It provides a detailed and fascinating look at the geology, plants, and historical sites along the route. The book is available in tourist shops and bookstores in Honolulu and on Kauaʻi.

Summer (May–October) is the best time of year to take this trip. The weather is usually drier then, the streams are easier to cross, and the beaches have lots of sand. Whenever you go, be prepared for rain and high water.

Bring a good tent and put all your dry gear in plastic bags. Pack a light sleeping bag or liner because the nights can be chilly, especially in winter. Take mosquito repellant if you plan to camp at Hanakoa. The dry, windy campsites at Kalalau Beach are relatively free of the pest. *Tabis* (Japanese reef walkers) with their fuzzy bottoms are perfect for exploring the slippery, rocky shoreline.

The driving instructions start from Līhuʻe Airport. All major rental car firms have booths there. Closer to the trailhead is Princeville Airport. From there you can take a taxi or hitchhike to the trailhead at Kē'ē Beach.

Coleman fuel (white gas) is available at 7-Eleven stores in Līhu'e and Kapa'a. Both towns have supermarkets with a wide selection of food items, as well as fuel.

The trailhead at Kē'ē Beach has restrooms, outside showers, and a water fountain where you can fill your water bottles. Unfortunately, break-ins are a common occurrence there; don't leave any valuables in your car.

Trailhead Directions

Distance: (Līhu'e Airport to Kē'ē Beach)—39 mi

Driving Time: 1 ¼ hr

Exit Līhu'e Airport on Ahukini Rd. (Rte 570).

At the first traffic light turn right on Kapule Hwy (Rte 51).

Kapule Hwy ends at the next major intersection. Continue straight on Kūhiō Hwy (Rte 56).

Cross the Wailua River on a bridge.

Drive through the town of Kapa'a.

Continue on Kūhiō Hwy along the windward coast.

Pass Kīlauea town on the right and cross a large bridge over Kalihiwai River.

Pass Princeville Airport on the left and Princeville resort on the right.

Descend into Hanalei Valley and cross the river on a long one-lane bridge.

Drive through Hanalei town.

Cross a series of short one-lane bridges.

Enter Hā'ena State Park.

Reach the end of the road at Kē'ē Beach (elev. 18 ft) (map point A). Park on either side of the road.

DAY ONE—Kē'ē Beach to Hanakoa Valley

Length: 6 mi

Elev. Gain/Loss: 1,200/750 ft

The route today is not long, but it does involve a series of elevation changes. The trail to Hanakāpī'ai Valley is wide, rutted, and well used by day hikers. Beyond the valley, the trail becomes more rough and narrow, but also less crowded. If you get a really late start, camp at Hanakāpī'ai, instead of Hanakoa.

Before starting, walk to Kē'ē Beach. A short hike along the beach to the right leads to a good first view of the Nā Pali Coast. To the left below the cliffs are the remains of a *heiau* (religious site) and a *hālau* (platform) where the ancient hula was performed.

The Nā Pali Coast–Kalalau Trail was originally an old Hawaiian route connecting the valleys along the coast. The trail was improved in the 1800s and the 1930s. The stone paving on the first section dates from that last upgrade.

About a half mile in is the first spectacular view of the Nā Pali Coast. Deep valleys alternate with vertical sea cliffs. Rainfall runoff created the valleys, and wave action, the cliffs. Where stream erosion has proceeded faster than sea erosion, the stream flows into the ocean at sea level, as at Hanakāpī'ai and Kalalau. The reverse situation creates a hanging valley with a waterfall cascading into the ocean, as at Hanakoa. From the view point you can also see the islands of Lehua and Ni'ihau in the distance.

The first valley you reach is Hanakāpī'ai (bay sprinkling food). It has several campsites, a curved white sand beach in summer, and a side trail leading into the valley to a waterfall. The stream is fast flowing and can rise suddenly. Do not cross it if the water is much above your knees.

The early Hawaiians settled in Hanakāpī'ai Valley. They lived near the beach and grew taro and other crops in rock terraces back in the valley. In the late 1800s Hanakāpī'ai was the site of a coffee plantation complete with a mill.

After climbing steeply out of Hanakāpī'ai Valley, the trail reaches its highest point above a small cove. The route then works into and out of two hanging valleys, Ho'olulu (protected bay) and Waiahuakua. The latter has several terraced sites near the trail but no signs of permanent habitation. In a cove below Waiahuakua is a beautiful sea cave, which, unfortunately, you cannot see from the trail.

The campground at Hanakoa (warrior bay) lies deep in the valley, well away from the coast. The best tent sites are in a terraced area under coffee bean trees on the far side of the stream. For obvious reasons, don't camp in or near the trashy, dilapidated shack. Wherever you camp, expect to be harassed by the resident mosquito population.

Water is from Hanakoa Stream and should be boiled, filtered, or chemically treated. There are small swimming holes both above and below the trail crossing. If you have time and energy after setting up camp, take the hike to lovely Hanakoa Falls. See tommorrow's narrative for directions.

Route Description:

The Nā Pali Coast–Kalalau Trail starts on the left just before the end of the paved road.

On the right pass a kiosk displaying maps and information about the trail.

Climb steadily along the Makana (gift) cliffs above Kēʻē Beach. The trail is very rocky and slippery when wet. Some sections are paved with smooth stones.

Work into and out of two small ravines. The first is dotted with hala trees, and the second, with kukui trees and ti plants.

Around the corner from the second ravine is the first good view of the Nā Pali Coast.

Work into and out of two more gulches. The last one has a small stream.

The trail straightens out for a while. Water seeps from the cliffs above.

Work into and out of another ravine.

Descend into a larger gulch on a series of switchbacks.

Cross a double stream and climb out of the gulch.

Descend into Hanakāpīʻai Valley on two switchbacks.

Pass a brown and yellow tsunami marker on the right.

Cross Hanakāpīʻai Stream (map point B). There is a rope strung across the stream for assistance. If the official ford doesn't appeal to you, walk toward the beach and cross where the stream is more wide and shallow.

Climb the opposite bank and turn sharp left upstream. (The faint trail to the right leads to several campsites and the beach.)

Shortly afterward reach a junction near a dilapidated shelter filled with trash. Keep right on the Nā Pali Coast–Kalalau Trail. (To the left the Hanakāpīʻai Falls Trail heads up Hanakāpīʻai Valley to the falls.)

Pass an elevated compost toilet on the right. Beyond the toilet is a picnic shelter.

Pass another tsunami marker on the right.

Climb out of Hanakāpīʻai Valley on 11 switchbacks. Along the trail are superb views of the beach and the valley.

Switch back six times up the cliffs along the coast.

Contour past a tiny pool at the base of a rock wall in a ravine. This area is known as Keanuenue (the rainbow).

Resume climbing on four switchbacks.

Reach the highest point on the trail by a huge boulder overlooking Hoʻolulu Valley (elev. 800 ft) (map point C). The sharp peak on the left is Pōhākea (white stone).

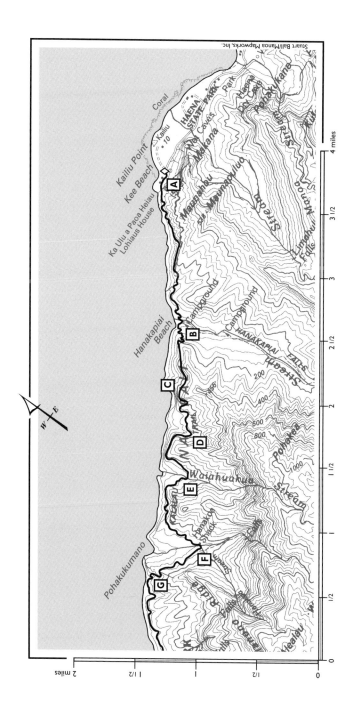

Stuart Ball/Manoa Mapworks, Inc.

Descend into Hoʻolulu Valley on a series of switchbacks.

Cross three tributaries of Hoʻolulu Stream.

Cross rocky, intermittent Hoʻolulu Stream (map point D).

Climb out of Hoʻolulu Valley.

Contour below near-vertical rock cliffs. Along the trail are good views back toward Kēʻē Beach.

Reach an overlook of Waiahuakua Valley.

Initially, climb into the valley and then descend on two switchbacks.

Cross three intermittent tributaries of Waiahuakua Stream.

Cross Waiahuakua Stream itself (map point E).

Cross two more intermittent tributaries.

Leaving the valley behind, climb steadily along sheer sea cliffs.

Ascend on two switchbacks.

Reach an overlook of Hanakoa Valley and Falls.

Descend very gradually into the valley.

Pass a mango tree on the right.

Pass a dilapidated shelter with a picnic table on the left.

Ford the two forks of Hanakoa Stream (elev. 450 ft) (map point F).

Set up camp at one of the sites on the left just after the stream crossing. Near the shelter are some alternate camping spots.

DAY TWO—Hanakoa Valley to Kalalau Beach

Length: 5 mi

Elev. Loss: 450 ft

Before leaving for Kalalau, take the short hike to Hanakoa Falls. The trail is little used and obscure in spots, but you should be able to follow it with these directions.

After crossing Hanakoa Stream, pass the first campsite.

Just before the second site, which is partially hidden, turn left on an obscure trail.

Climb over several rock walls and bear left.

Cross the right fork of Hanakoa Stream.

Gradually ascend the ridge between the two forks of Hanakoa Stream.

Work left to parallel the left fork of the stream.

Cross a side stream and climb steeply.

By a mango tree continue to follow the left fork, but continue well above it.

Descend to stream level and, shortly afterward, reach Hanakoa Falls.

The back of Hanakoa Valley resembles a huge amphitheater. At the center is a circular pool, perhaps the largest in the state. Ringing the pool are four vertical waterfall chutes. Hanakoa Falls cascades down the chute on the right, which is usually the only one with water. Try the long swim to the base of the falls. Look for koaʻe, the white-tailed tropic bird, as it soars along the cliffs above. Enjoy the wild, rugged beauty of this remote spot.

The route to Kalalau on the main trail is short and generally downhill. After Hanakoa, the country becomes more dry and open with breathtaking views all around. Don't hike and look at the same time, however, because the trail has some very narrow and eroded spots with loose rock.

After the series of eroded sections, the route crosses a level area covered with scrub guava and lantana. The Hawaiians used to grow taro here. In the next gulch you find taro and ʻape, with its oversize heart-shaped leaves. It is a close relative of taro. Also in the gulch are lama trees with dark green, leathery leaves. The hard, light-colored wood was sacred to the Hawaiians. They used it in temple construction and in hula performances.

In the next gulch you can easily recognize sisal by its swordlike leaves. They used to be made into rope, and the plant was introduced into Hawaiʻi in the late 1800s for that purpose. Sisal puts up a tall flower stalk every 10 years or so where the baby plants form.

The first spectacular view of Kalalau (the straying) Beach and Valley is from Puʻukula overlook. There, you may also see some feral goats, which are responsible for the denuded hillsides nearby. From the lookout, descend to Kalalau Stream very carefully as the footing is treacherous on the loose red dirt. The stream is fast flowing and can rise suddenly. Do not cross it if the water is much above your knees.

The campsites at Kalalau are strung along the half-mile beach. At the near east end of the beach by a helipad are some shady, secluded sites. Toward the middle of the beach the sites are more exposed and sociable. In summer you can even camp in the cave at the far west end of the beach. The sites near the cliffs look attractive, but sometimes they get bombarded with small and not so small rocks. Wherever you camp, make sure you have some nearby shade as the afternoon sun can be hot.

The campground has the usual dilapidated shelters and three elevated compost toilets spaced evenly behind the beach. Water is available from Kalalau Stream or from Hoʻoleʻa Falls near the far end of the beach. Boil, filter, or chemically treat the water, as always. The waterfall also makes an excellent shower.

Swim in the ocean only in summer. Even then, be careful as the waves and currents are very powerful. Keep in mind that the Nā Pali Coast is subject to tsunami (sea waves) generated by earthquakes. If you feel one, or the ocean starts to recede, move to high ground immediately.

Route Description:

Climb gradually out of Hanakoa Valley.

Cross over the end of Manono Ridge. There are good views along the coast in both directions; Kalalau, however, remains hidden by the intervening cliffs.

Descend into a gulch on 10 switchbacks (map point G). The trail, narrow in spots, hugs the cliff above the ocean.

Work into and out of two more gulches. In the second one cross a tiny stream and switch back several times.

Reach a windy, grassy overlook.

Descend into and climb out of another gulch. The trail crosses a stream and is deeply eroded in some sections.

Reach a bare lookout. Way to the left below the cliffs is a narrow, inaccessible beach.

Traverse an eroded, crumbly section. The trail is narrow in spots.

Descend into and climb out of a deep ravine with a fast-flowing stream.

Contour through scrub guava and lantana. Look for a sea arch below.

Descend into a deep, lush gulch (map point H). Lining the stream are taro and 'ape. Along the sides of the ravine are lama trees.

While climbing out of the gulch, pass a rock wall on the left.

Cross a hot, dry gulch dotted with sisal.

Contour around the back of two small ravines.

Descend into a larger gulch and cross a stream. Turn left uphill, paralleling the stream.

By a small waterfall switch back to the right and climb out of the gulch.

Reach an overlook. Below is a rock with a double hole. Above are the rocky, turreted ridges of the Nā Pali Coast.

Contour around the back of a deep, narrow ravine.

Work into and out of a gulch lined with kukui trees.

Reach another lookout. The narrow ridges above are near vertical.

Traverse a series of small, ill-defined gulches.

Reach a grassy eroded overlook known as Pu'ukula near the end of Ka'a'alahina Ridge (map point I). To the left is the broad expanse of Kalalau Beach and behind it, Kalalau Valley. Above is massive Kanakou peak.

Descend a red, eroded slope, gradually at first and then more steeply. The trail is washed out in spots and deeply grooved in others.

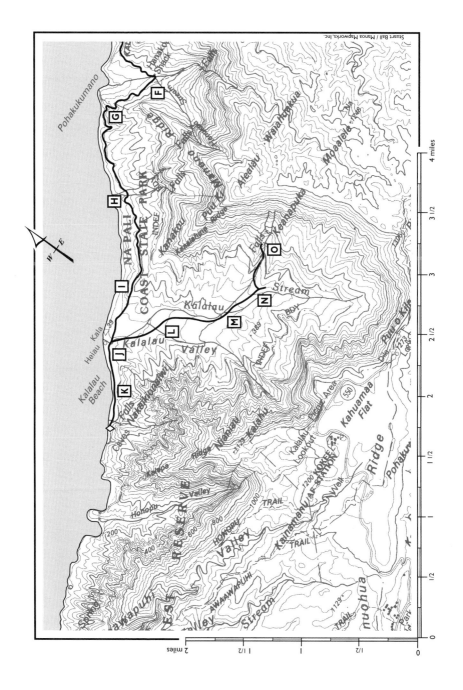

At the bottom of the slope bear left through a grassy area.

The trail winds through a forest of Java plum.

Descend steeply to Kalalau Stream.

Ford the stream where it splits to form an island. A rope is provided for assistance.

Turn right downstream.

Climb the bank, angling away from the stream.

Reach a signed junction (map point J). Turn right, toward the beach. (To the left is the Kalalau Valley Trail, which leads into the valley and is the route for tomorrow's day hike.)

Reach the shore and turn left along the vegetation line.

Cross an intermittent stream.

Begin passing turnoffs to campsites in the trees on the left.

Pass an open, grassy area used as a helipad.

Pass a turnoff to an elevated compost toilet and a trash pit.

The trail splits (map point K). The left fork leads to a series of campsites below the cliffs. The right fork goes straight to the beach.

DAY THREE—Day hike to Big Pool and Waimakemake Falls

Length: 4.5 mi

Elev. Gain/Loss: 1,500/1,500 ft

The hike today up-valley involves some elevation gain, but the climb is gradual. The route to Big Pool is wide open and easy to follow. The trail to Waimakemake Falls is narrower, rougher, and obscure in spots.

Big Pool is not that big, but it is deep, and the water is cool and inviting. Its setting is idyllic, nestled below two miniature waterfalls and the towering west wall of the valley. The rock slabs next to the pool are perfect for stretching out on.

Along the way to Big Pool you pass through several terraced areas, now overgrown with Java plum and other introduced trees. The rock walls originally enclosed taro patches, cultivated by the Hawaiians. They transported their crop by canoe along the coast to trade for other staples. The Hawaiians used the wood from the tangled hau trees along the trail to make the outriggers for their narrow canoes.

After a refreshing dip at Big Pool, backtrack down the valley trail for about five minutes to the junction with the falls trail. It is not well marked. Look for a collapsed rock wall on the left and a guava tree with two rusty nails on the right.

Waimakemake consists of two upper falls and one lower one. The trail reaches the base of the lower cascade with its tiny pool. The falls are fed by springs in the cliffs above. Vertical rock dikes trap water in the porous lava and release it over the falls. Waimakemake is also known as Davis Falls, named after Richard H. Davis, mountain man and explorer from the Hawaiian Trail and Mountain Club on O'ahu.

On the way back to your campsite take a short side trip to the *heiau* on the bluff between Kalalau Stream and Beach. At the junction with the coast trail, turn right toward the stream. Almost immediately, turn left on a faint trail through some boulders. Climb gradually to a grass-covered plateau with the remains of a *heiau* on top. To get back to the beach, descend the front of the plateau and turn left.

Back at the beach make the most of the rest of the afternoon. Sunbathe. Take a swim or a snooze. Just enjoy the stunning view of blue ocean, white sand, and red, black, and green cliffs. In the evening watch the sun set over the Pacific Ocean, and the stars come out. Life doesn't get much better than this!

Route Description:

Retrace your steps to the junction just before Kalalau Stream (map point J). Continue straight, on the Kalalau Valley Trail. (The trail to the left is the familiar Nā Pali Coast–Kalalau Trail.)

Climb gradually up the valley past tangled hau trees.

Keep to the left in a rocky eroded area.

Ascend steadily through mixed exotic forest.

Skirt to the left of another eroded section.

Cross a dry stream bed in a hau grove.

Go through an area terraced with rock walls.

Cross a tributary of Kalalau Stream (map point L).

Climb the opposite bank and turn sharp right.

Ascend steadily past more terraces.

Break out into the open briefly through guava and lantana.

Pass several large mango trees.

Cross another tributary of Kalalau Stream.

Continue climbing past a hau grove.

A series of mango trees lines the trail.

Cross Kalalau Stream (map point M).

Ascend through another terraced area and then through a hau tangle.

Reach an obscure junction marked by two rusty nails in a guava tree near a collapsed rock wall (map point N). For now, continue straight on the valley trail. (The trail to the left leads to Waimakemake Falls and is the extended portion of today's hike.) Memorize the junction for the return trip.

Parallel a brook on the right.

Cross the brook and turn left.

Kalalau Stream comes in on the right. Follow it upstream.

Reach Big Pool just below some rock slabs (elev. 900 ft). Jump in! Above Big Pool are two tiny cascading waterfalls. From the pool are good views of the back and west wall of Kalalau Valley.

After swimming, retrace your steps to the obscure junction (map point N). Turn right on the trail to Waimakemake Falls. (If you've had enough hiking for today, continue straight, back to the beach.)

Go through a rock wall and turn right.

Cross the stream flowing from Waimakemake Falls and turn right upstream.

Work left, following the stream, but well above it.

Pass a huge mango tree on the left.

Break out into the open briefly through grass.

Descend to the stream, cross it, and turn left upstream.

Climb well above the stream, but still paralleling it.

Descend to the stream.

Angle up a steep rock slab with the aid of a rope.

Climb steeply past a small waterfall on the left.

Cross the stream and bear right upstream.

Ascend steeply past a second smaller waterfall on the right.

Reach the base of Waimakemake Falls (elev. 1,500 ft) (map point O).

Backtrack to the junction with the valley trail (map point N). Turn left for another swim or turn right for the beach.

DAY FOUR—Kalalau Beach to Kēʻē Beach

Length: 11 mi

Elev. Gain/Loss: 1,200/1,200 ft

Retrace your steps to Kēʻē Beach. Start early to avoid the hot sun during the steep climb out of Kalalau Valley.

Options:

Most variations of this trip involve the time spent, rather than the route. The minimum stay is two days, one in and one out, but don't even think of doing the trip in that short a time. You are going to be very tired and very disappointed that you didn't spend an extra day at Kalalau. The trip as described is a leisurely four days, two in and one out with one layover day. The maximum allowable stay is currently six days. Novice backpackers can camp at Hanakāpīʻai or even Hanakoa and then return the next day. That short, two-day trip avoids most of the narrow spots but still provides a good introduction to the Nā Pali Coast. Kalalau is a wilderness Waikīkī. It's crowded, noisy, and a bit trashy, but still great fun. If you are looking for more solitude, try the other coastal trips, Waimanu Valley, Kaʻaha, or even Halapē.

7. Mōhihi-Koaiʻe

Type:	Mountain
Length:	2–3 days, 19.6 mi round trip
Elev. Gain/Loss:	1,400/1,400 ft
Difficulty:	Low
Location:	Kauaʻi: Kōkeʻe State Park, Nā Pali–Kona Forest Reserve, Alakaʻi Wilderness Preserve
Topo Map:	Hāʻena, Waimea Canyon

Highlights

A pleasant road walk near Waimea Canyon turns into a wilderness hike through the Alakaʻi Swamp. The destination is a remote camp a few miles from Waiʻaleʻale, the highest mountain on Kauaʻi and the wettest spot on earth. Along the way are wild, scenic overlooks, surging streams, and a rich variety of native rain forest plants.

Planning

Call or write the Kauaʻi Division of Forestry for a trail map and camping permit information. The phone number is (808) 241–3433, and the address is 3060 ʻEiwa St., Līhuʻe, HI 96766.

Summer (May–October) is the best time of year to take this trip. The weather is usually drier then, and the streams are easier to cross. Whenever you go, be prepared for rain and cool temperatures. Bring a light sleeping bag and a tent that keeps you dry in a heavy downpour.

The driving instructions start from Līhuʻe Airport. All major rental car firms have booths there.

Coleman fuel (white gas) is available at 7-Eleven stores in Līhuʻe and Kapaʻa. Both towns have supermarkets with a wide selection of food items, as well as fuel. You can fill your water bottles near the trailhead in Kōkeʻe State Park.

Trailhead Directions

Distance: (Līhuʻe Airport to Kōkeʻe campground) —40 mi

Driving Time: 1 ½ hr

74

Exit Līhu'e Airport on Ahukini Rd. (Rte 570).

Continue straight across the intersection with Kapule Hwy.

Ahukini Rd. ends. Turn left on Kūhiō Hwy (Rte 56).

Drive through Līhu'e town.

Turn right on Kaumuali'i Hwy (Rte 50).

Pass a sugar mill on the left.

Pass Kaua'i Community College on the right.

Drive through sugar cane fields.

Pass the towns of Lāwa'i and Kalāheo.

Pass the Hanapēpē River overlook on the right.

Drive through the towns of 'Ele'ele and Hanapēpē.

Pass the Russian fort on the left.

Enter Waimea town.

Look for the Waimea Baptist Church on the right. It's beige with a white steeple.

Just past the church, turn right on Waimea Canyon Rd.

Ascend gradually along the rim of Waimea Canyon.

At the stop sign turn right on Kōke'e Rd.

Pass the Kōke'e Hunter Check-in Station on the right.

Pass turnoffs to Waimea Canyon and Pu'u Hinahina lookouts on the right.

Enter Kōke'e State Park.

Pass the Kōke'e cabins on the left.

By the park headquarters turn left to Kōke'e Lodge and Museum. Fill your water bottles at the picnic pavilion just beyond the museum.

Drive back to the main road and turn left on it.

Take the first left to Kōke'e campground and park in the lot there (elev. 3,680 ft) (map point A).

DAY ONE—Kōke'e campground to Sugi Grove

Length: 3.5 mi

Elev. Loss: 200 ft

Today's route is easy; the mileage is low, and the walking is all on dirt roads. Don't start too late, however, because one of the finest stream hikes in Hawai'i awaits you at Sugi Grove.

Before starting out, spend some time at Kōke'e Museum. It has excellent exhibits on the area's plants, animals, and geology. Look for *Koke'e Trails*, an informative brochure and trail map.

The Alaka'i Picnic Area makes a good lunch spot. From its overlook you can see down Po'omau Canyon and up toward the peak of Wai'ale'ale.

Camp either at Sugi Grove or Kawaikōī Camp. Sugi Grove is less crowded, but during heavy rains water puddles in the low-lying areas of the camp. Pick your tent site carefully. Both camps have pit toilets and covered picnic tables. Water is available from Kawaikōī Stream. Boil, filter, or chemically treat it. Sugi Grove is a large stand of Japanese sugi cedars, which were planted in the 1930s by the Civilian Conservation Corps.

After setting up camp, take a short stroll on the Kawaikōī Stream Trail. It starts across the road from Sugi Grove and follows the south bank of the stream. Farther in is a more difficult loop section that crosses the stream twice.

The Kawaikōī Stream Trail is perhaps the most lovely and serene stream hike in Hawai'i. The water flowing by is dark, mysterious, and comes from deep in the Alaka'i Swamp. Savor this walk; don't rush it.

Route Description:

Walk back to Kōke'e Rd. and turn left on it.

Almost immediately turn right on a dirt road that splits three ways. Take the middle fork, which is Camp 10–Mōhihi Rd. (The left fork goes to a private cabin and the right, to a water tank.)

Descend gradually under a canopy of koa trees.

A well-used dirt road comes in on the right (map point B). Keep left.

The road is lined with eucalyptus trees. On both sides are driveways leading to private cabins.

The road forks. Take the right fork, still on Camp 10–Mōhihi Rd. (The left fork leads to the Pu'u Ka'ōhelo–Berry Flat Trail.)

Climb gradually and go through an open yellow gate.

At the next fork, keep left on Camp 10–Mōhihi Rd (map point C). (To the right is the Kumuwela Rd., leading to the Canyon and Ditch Trails.)

Cross a flat area. The Pu'u Ka'ōhelo-Berry Flat Trail comes in on the left.

The road forks again. Keep left on the main route.

Shortly afterward the road turns right and begins to descend.

Parallel a tributary of Kauaikanana Stream.

As the road turns sharp left, it splits. Keep left on the main route. (The road to the right leads down to Kauaikanana Stream and the Ditch Trail.)

Cross Kauaikanana Stream on a bridge (map point D).

Cross a tributary of Kauaikanana Stream on another bridge.

After climbing steadily, reach a signed junction. Continue straight on

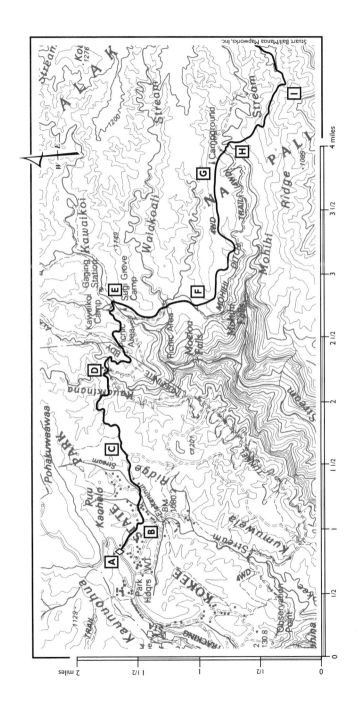

Camp 10–Mōhihi Rd. (The grassy road to the left is the start of the Alaka'i Trail that leads to the Alaka'i Swamp and the Pihea Trail. The grassy road to the right leads a short distance to the Alaka'i Picnic Area. It has a covered table, pit toilet, and a superb view down Po'omau Canyon.)

Descend gradually toward Kawaikōī Stream.

Pass Kawaikōī Camp and picnic area on the left.

Ford Kawaikōī Stream.

Shortly afterward reach a junction. Turn right into Sugi Grove and camp (elev. 3,440 ft) (map point E). (To the left is tomorrow's route along Camp 10–Mōhihi Rd.)

DAY TWO—Sugi Grove to Koai'e Camp

Length: 6.3 mi

Elev. Gain/Loss: 800/400 ft

The route today initially follows Camp 10 Rd. to its end. From there the Mōhihi–Wai'alae Trail takes you across Mōhihi Stream, up Kohua Ridge, and into the Alaka'i Swamp. The trail is well maintained and even has a bench and mileage markers. How civilized can you get?

Except for sugi cedars and blackberry, the vegetation along the trail is all native. On the lower, drier section of the ridge are the shrubs 'a'ali'i and naupaka kuahiwi. 'A'ali'i has narrow leaves and red seed capsules. You can recognize naupaka by its white, half-formed flowers.

The most common tree is 'ōhi'a lehua with its clusters of delicate red flowers. Also present is mokihana, found only on Kaua'i. It has oblong leaves with blunt tips. When crushed, they give off a strong anise scent.

Farther along the ridge you begin to see 'ōlapa and lapalapa. They are small trees with pale green leaves that flutter in the slightest wind. The leaves of lapalapa are almost round, while those of 'ōlapa are more oblong.

Look for two native birds, 'elepaio and 'anianiau. 'Elepaio is brown on top and whitish underneath with a dark tail, usually cocked. Found only on Kaua'i, 'anianiau is yellow-green on top and bright yellow underneath with a short, slightly curved bill. Both birds are very curious, which is why you can often see them.

Gradually, Kohua Ridge turns into an arm of the Alaka'i Swamp. The ground becomes spongy and muddy with some pools of standing water. Hapu'u tree ferns form a nearly continuous understory in the 'ōhi'a rain forest.

The final descent to Koai'e Stream and Camp is short, but steep, and can be very slippery. Take your time and watch your footing. Do not cross Koai'e Stream if the water is much above your knees. If necessary, climb back up the ridge and camp on top.

Koai'e Camp has four to five good tent sites. Water is available from Koai'e Stream. Boil, filter, or chemically treat the water, as usual. There is no toilet so bury your waste well away from the stream. The dilapidated shack at the camp is small, damp, and dirty; don't depend on it for shelter.

If you have time and energy after setting up camp, explore a ways along the ridge above. To get there, walk away from the stream and shack, keeping the tent sites on your left. By a large fallen tree, bear right and up. Cross a short muddy section covered with blackberry. Begin climbing steeply up the ridge. To the right are good views down Koai'e Canyon. This trail is not maintained.

Koai'e Camp is a wet and wild place. The lush, dense rain forest is all around and is constantly dripping. Rain comes often, usually in the afternoon and at night. Mist settles in the canyon and mingles with the dark, rushing water in the stream.

Route Description:

Walk back to Camp 10–Mōhihi Rd. and turn right on it.

Almost immediately reach a signed junction. Stick to the road. (To the left the Kawaikōī Stream Trail loops around the stream and connects with the Pihea Trail.)

The road climbs and then descends.

Pass the turnoff to Waiakoali Picnic Area on the right. Keep left on the main road.

Ford Waiakoali Stream.

Reach a major intersection (map point F). Continue straight across and up on Camp 10–Mōhihi Rd. (To the left and right a dirt road parallels an irrigation ditch.)

Reach a signed junction. Stick to the road. (To the right the Po'omau Canyon Vista Trail leads a short distance to a lookout.)

Climb steadily, cross a flat area and then descend.

Reach another signed junction. Keep to the road. (To the right the Kohua Ridge Trail descends a side ridge with views of Po'omau and Koai'e Canyons.)

Reach a fork. Keep left uphill, still on Camp 10–Mōhihi Rd. (The right fork leads down to Mōhihi Ditch.)

The road climbs gradually and then levels off.

Reach the end of Camp 10–Mōhihi Rd. at a picnic area (map point G).

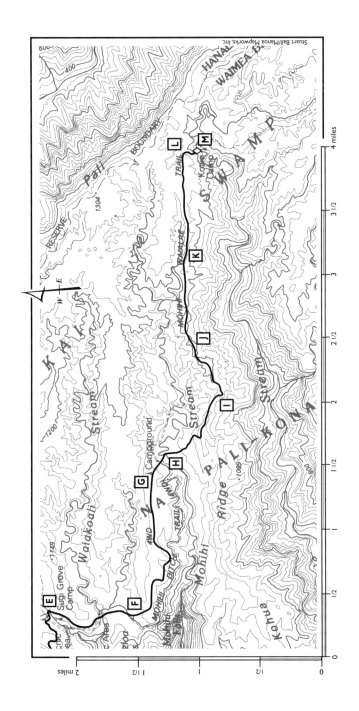

Pick up the Mōhihi–Wai'alae Trail just past the covered table.

Initially, the trail is a grassy road that descends.

Cross Mōhihi Ditch on a small bridge.

Sign in at the brown trail register across the road. To the left is a covered picnic area.

Descend steeply on a trail toward Mōhihi Stream.

Ford the stream and turn left upstream (map point H).

Shortly afterward and before reaching a gaging station on the right, turn sharp right on the Mōhihi–Wai'alae Trail.

Leaving the stream behind, ascend steeply up a side ridge.

Descend briefly and then resume the ascent through sugi cedars.

Climb steeply. The trail attempts to switchback occasionally.

Reach the top of Kohua Ridge and bear left. Except for blackberry, the trees and shrubs along the ridge are all native. They include 'ōhi'a lehua, 'ōlapa, lapalapa, mokihana, 'akoko, 'a'ali'i, naupaka kuahiwi, and lobelia.

Ascend gradually along the ridge.

Descend and then climb steeply to a knoll with a bench (map point I). From it are views down Koai'e Canyon to Waimea Canyon.

The trail works to the left side of the ridge as it widens.

Go through several thickets of blackberry. Watch out for the thorns!

Climb steadily with one short descent.

Reach a grassy knoll with a rain gauge (map point J). Bear right around the knoll.

Climb steadily as the ridge narrows.

The trail drops off the ridge line to the right several times to avoid narrow or overgrown sections.

On the left pass a vertical cliff with ferns growing on it.

The trail swings left. Enter the lush native rain forest, dominated by hapu'u tree ferns.

Bear right off the ridge top under a cliff. Climb steeply to regain the ridge line.

The ridge widens, flattens, and becomes an arm of the Alaka'i Swamp (map point K).

Wind through dripping forest, mud holes, and pools of standing water for a long stretch.

Turn sharp right down a side ridge toward Koai'e Stream (map point L).

The trail hugs the left side of the ridge, initially.

Descend steeply and cross a gully.

Descend right and then left, very steeply.

Reach Koai'e Stream and ford it.

Climb the opposite bank and turn left upstream.
Pass a dilapidated shack on the left.
In back of the shack is Koai'e Camp (elev. 3,880 ft) (map point M).

DAY THREE—Koai'e Camp to Kōke'e campground

Length: 9.8 mi

Elev. Gain/Loss: 600/800 ft

Retrace your steps back to Kōke'e campground.

Options:

Variations of this trip are few and less than attractive. Groups with limited time can make a two-day trip by hiking to Koai'e Camp on the first day. Unfortunately, you miss camping at Sugi Grove and walking the idyllic Kawaikōī Stream Trail.

Parties with an extra day could spend it at Koai'e Camp, poking around the swamp and enjoying the swimming hole. That would make a pleasant day if the weather is any good, but it rarely is.

MAUI

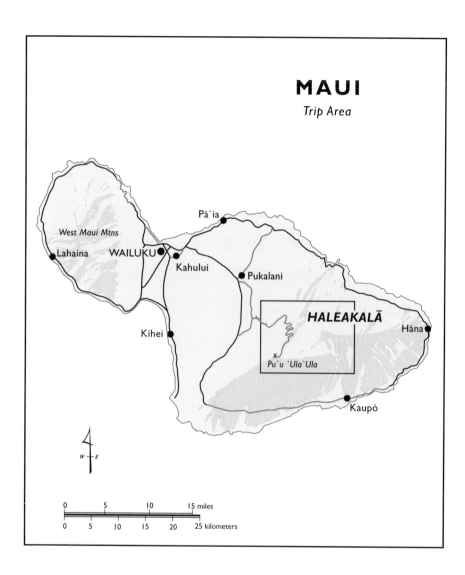

MAUI

Trip Area

West Maui Mtns

Lahaina

WAILUKU

Kahului

Pā`ia

Pukalani

HALEAKALĀ

Kīhei

x
Pu`u `Ula`Ula

Hāna

Kaupō

W — E

0   5   10   15 miles

0   5   10   15   20   25 kilometers

8. Haleakalā

Type:	Mountain
Length:	2–4 days, 20.0 mi loop
Elev. Gain/Loss:	2,400/4,200 ft
Difficulty:	Medium
Location:	Maui: Haleakalā National Park
Topo Map:	Kilohana, Nāhiku

Highlights

Haleakalā (house of the sun) is a once active volcano with a vast eroded crater, much like an amphitheater. On this loop trip through the crater, you see towering cliffs, colorful spatter cones, and dark lava tubes. Much in evidence are two threatened species, nēnē, the Hawaiian goose, and 'āhinahina, the Haleakalā silversword.

Planning

Call or write the National Park for a brochure, trail map, and camping information. The Park Headquarters phone number is (808) 572–9306, and the address is Superintendent, Haleakalā National Park, P.O. Box 369, Makawao, HI 96798. There is also a recording of general park information at (808) 572–7749.

You can take this trip any time during the year. Winter (November–April) is predictably rainier and colder than summer (May–October). Be prepared for large temperature swings. At night the thermometer drops to the thirties in winter and forties in summer at Hōlua. On a sunny day the crater warms up quickly to the seventies or eighties.

Bring a three-season sleeping bag and four layers of clothing. The outer layer should protect you from wind and rain. Include gloves or mittens and a hat or balaclava.

The driving instructions start from Kahului Airport. All major rental car firms have booths there.

Coleman fuel (white gas) is available at 7-Eleven Stores and major supermarkets in Kahului. You can also find fuel at Foodland Super Market in Pukalani on the drive up to the National Park.

Stop at Park Headquarters to pick up a backcountry use permit.

Headquarters is open from 7:30 A.M. to 4 P.M. daily. Fill your water bottles there for the first day as the trailhead has a limited supply.

The trip narrative assumes you are staying at the campgrounds each night. There are, however, three cabins in the crater at Kapalaoa, Palikū, and Hōlua. Each has 12 bunks with mattresses, a table and chairs, and a kitchen area with a sink and wood cookstove. Nearby outside are a water tank and a pit toilet. The cabins are very comfortable and very popular. If you're interested, write to the above address 90 days in advance of your trip. State your first choice of dates and cabins and then include some alternates. The Park Service conducts a monthly lottery to select the winners. Good luck!

Trailhead Directions

Distance: (Kahului Airport to Sliding Sands trailhead)—37 mi

Driving Time: 1 ¼ hr

Exit Kahului Airport on Keolani Pl. (Rte 380).

At the first traffic light turn left on Hāna Hwy (Rte 36). (To the right Rte 36 leads into Kahului town.)

At the next major intersection turn right on Haleakalā Hwy (Rte 37). Ascend gradually through sugar cane fields.

Pass turnoffs to Pukalani on the right and Makawao on the left.

The highway narrows to two lanes.

Turn left on Rte 377 (still Haleakalā Hwy).

Climb steadily through lush pasture land and stands of fragrant eucalyptus trees.

Pass Kula Lodge on the right.

Turn left on Haleakalā Crater Rd. (Rte 378).

Ascend steeply on a series of short switchbacks through pasture land belonging to Haleakalā Ranch.

Enter Haleakalā National Park and pay the fee at the entrance station.

Pass a road leading to Hosmer Grove campground on the left.

Stop at Park Headquarters on the right (elev. 7,030 ft). There, get a backcountry permit for the trip and ask about current trail conditions. Remember to fill your water bottles.

On the left pass the parking area for Halemau'u trailhead (elev. 7,990 ft) (map point T). The trip ends there.

Pass Leleiwi and Kalahaku overlooks, both on the left.

Turn left into the parking area for Haleakalā Visitor Center. Park your car in the near right corner of the lot close to a horse loading ramp (elev. 9,780 ft) (map point A). If you have two cars, drop off people and packs and shuttle one car back to Halemauʻu trailhead.

DAY ONE—Visitor Center to Palikū

Length: 9.8 mi

Elev. Loss: 3,400 ft

Start early today so you have time to enjoy the scenery. The route is long, but the trail is well graded and all downhill. The initial high altitude should not cause any major problems because of the quick descent to a much lower elevation.

From Haleakalā Visitor Center is the first panoramic view of the crater. To the northeast, below Leleiwi Pali, is Hōlua Cabin. Beyond is Koʻolau Gap, descending to the north coast of Maui. To the east is today's route through the crater. At its far end lies Palikū below the green crater wall. To the right of Palikū and out of sight is Kaupō Gap, descending to the south coast of the island.

Haleakalā is a dormant volcano, but its "crater" is not really a volcanic one. The vast double amphitheater below you is more the result of wind and water erosion than volcanic activity. From opposite sides of the island two streams eroded headward and met to form a "crater." Lava from vents near the summit partially filled both deep valleys to create the wide Koʻolau and Kaupō Gaps. More recent volcanic activity produced the colorful spatter cones dotting the crater floor. Haleakalā erupted for perhaps the last time in 1790. In that eruption two small flows from the southwest rift zone outside the crater reached the ocean.

Once in the crater the first plant you see is ʻāhinahina, the Haleakalā silversword. It has narrow silver-green leaves and a tall flower stalk. The leaves are covered with tiny hairs to conserve moisture and protect the plant from the intense sun. Other adaptations include a deep tap root to anchor the plant in high winds and a wide network of surface roots to collect water. The silversword usually grows for 15 to 20 years before flowering. The flower stalks usually appear in summer or early fall and have purple blossoms. After the seeds develop, the entire plant dies. Silverswords are endemic to Hawaiʻi, meaning they are found nowhere else. Don't approach mature plants too closely, and don't step on the baby ones!

At Kapalaoa Cabin you may see your first nēnē, the Hawaiian goose. Some like to hang around the cabins so look for them at Palikū and Hōlua, too. The nēnē has a black face and head and a gray-brown body. It lives on dry, rugged lava flows at high elevation and so has lost much of the webbing on its feet. Like its Canadian counterpart, the nēnē is a strong flyer and often honks in mid-flight. The nēnē is a threatened species and should be treated with respect and awe.

Between Kapalaoa and Palikū Cabins the vegetation gradually reappears. It's mostly native dry-land shrubs, including pūkiawe, 'a'ali'i, pilo, and 'ōhelo. Pūkiawe has narrow rigid leaves and small white, pink, or red berries. 'A'ali'i has shiny leaves and red seed capsules. Pilo is low lying with orange berries. 'Ōhelo has rounded leaves and juicy yellow-red berries, about the size of blueberries. Both nēnē and hikers love 'ōhelo berries. Try them; they are especially delicious ice cold in the morning.

The campground at Palikū is a grassy field on the left just before the cabin. The water supply is from a faucet on the trail to the cabin. Boil, filter, or chemically treat the water. The pit toilet is behind the cabin.

Palikū is a very special place. The pasture and towering *pali* (cliff) are so lush and green after the colorful, but desolate, walk across the crater. Evenings at Palikū are magical. Watch the lingering color of the sunset on the cliffs and clouds above Kaupō Gap. Listen for the honk of a pair of nēnē making their last flight of the evening. Look for the moon rising through a notch in the crater wall. Can life get any better than this?

In Hawaiian, Haleakalā means house of the sun. According to legend, the sun traveled so quickly across the sky that the farmers and fishermen did not have enough time to plant crops and catch fish before night fell. The demigod, Māui, went to Haleakalā where the sun's rays first struck the island. There Māui snared the sun with 16 great ropes. In return for his freedom the sun promised to travel more slowly across the sky. Māui let the sun go but left some ropes tied to the sun to remind him of his promise. The people now had more time to catch fish and grow their crops. At sunset you can still see the white ropes trailing through the sky.

Route Description:

The Sliding Sands Trail starts by a wooden bulletin board next to the horse loading ramp.

Briefly parallel the paved road leading to Pu'u 'Ula'ula (Red Hill), the summit of Haleakalā at 10,023 ft.

Bear left away from the road around Pakao'ao (White Hill).

Reach the rim of the crater and the first of many awesome views.

Descend gradually on five long, lazy switchbacks. The trail crosses an

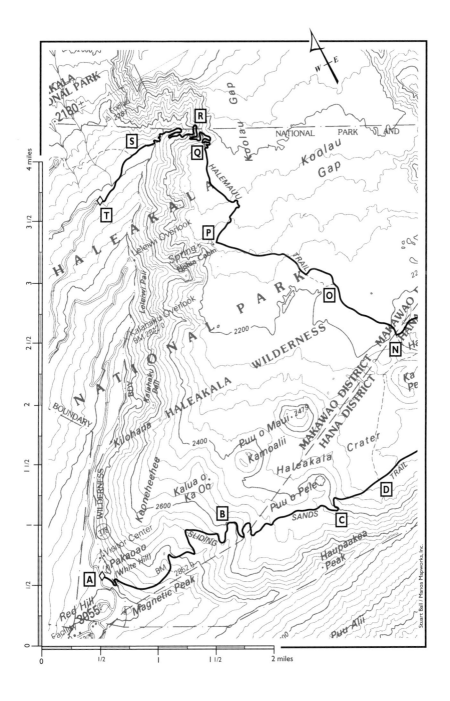

area of grey-brown and then red-brown cinders known as keonehe'ehe'e (sliding sands).

Pass a group of silverswords on the right. The only other vegetation in the vicinity is scattered pūkiawe and kūpaoa.

Reach a signed junction (map point B). Turn right, between two boulders and a lone 'ōhelo. The side trail straight ahead leads down to a view into Kalu'uoka'ō'ō (the plunge of the digging stick) cone.

Continue the descent on three switchbacks. The trail briefly crosses rough 'a'ā lava. Watch your footing on the loose rock.

Pass a patch of silverswords.

Cross a relatively flat area covered with red cinder. Silverswords line the trail. Kama'oli'i (small native cotton bush) and Pu'u o Māui (hill of Māui) cones are on the left at a distance.

Pass Pu'u o Pele (hill of Pele), a red cinder cone, close by on the left.

Descend to the crater floor on two switchbacks (map point C).

Reach a signed junction by a hitching post and a māmane tree (map point D). Continue straight on the Sliding Sands Trail. (The side trail to the left leads across the crater to Halemau'u Trail and Hōlua Cabin and campground.)

The main trail straightens out and is wide and sandy in spots.

Pass more silverswords on the left. Well behind them is Kamoa o Pele (the chicken of Pele), a large red cinder cone.

Cross a field of kīlau (bracken) ferns and native bunch grass.

Reach an obscure junction (map point E). Again, continue straight toward Kapalaoa Cabin. (The side trail to the left leads across the crater to Halemau'u Trail and Hōlua Cabin and campground.)

Reach another signed junction. Continue straight on the main trail. (The side trail to the left leads across the crater to Halemau'u Trail and Hōlua Cabin and campground.)

Almost immediately, reach Kapalaoa (the sperm whale) Cabin (map point F). Water is available from a tank in back. Boil, filter, or chemically treat the water. No tent camping is allowed.

After leaving the cabin, the vegetation gradually reappears. You can see pūkiawe, 'ōhelo, 'a'ali'i, and pilo.

Wind through an 'a'ā lava flow on a rough trail. It briefly parallels an eroded gully on the right.

Work left around Pu'u Maile (maile hill), a vegetated cone.

Descend steadily through broken-up 'a'ā lava (map point G). Watch for loose rock on the trail. Look for a lone 'iliahi (sandalwood) on the right.

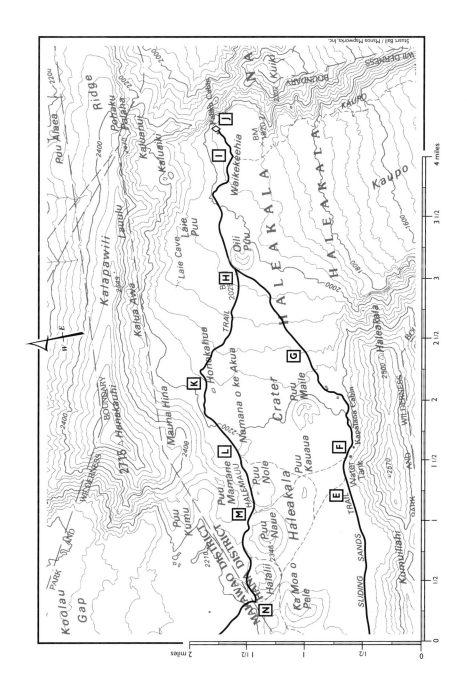

Cross a mostly barren ʻaʻā flow.

Go left around a vegetated cone, known as ʻŌʻilipuʻu (hill appearing).

Reach a signed junction with the Halemauʻu (grass house) Trail (map point H). Turn right on it toward Palikū (vertical cliff). (To the left is the route tomorrow to Hōlua campground.)

Continue around the base of the cone.

Descend gradually on old pāhoehoe lava through pūkiawe and ʻōhelo.

Reach a signed junction (map point I). Keep left to Palikū. (The trail to the right leads down Kaupō [landing at night] Gap to the town of Kaupō along the south coast.)

Reach Palikū campground and cabin (elev. 6,380 ft) (map point J).

DAY TWO—Palikū to Hōlua

Length: 6.3 mi

Elev. Gain/Loss: 1,000/400 ft

If you wish, linger at Palikū for awhile this morning. The route today does not require a crack-of-dawn start; the mileage is low, and the trail is well marked and groomed. The hike is a gradual climb to Bottomless Pit and then a gradual descent to Hōlua campground.

The route to Hōlua recrosses the crater along its northern side. You get to see several of the large cones and deep pits up close, rather than from a distance as you did yesterday. Along the way the vegetation pattern begins with native shrubs near Palikū, switches to silverswords among the cones, and reverts to native shrubs near Hōlua.

Hōlua campground enjoys a spectacular setting at the top of Koʻolau Gap and at the foot of Leleiwi Pali. There are numerous flat tent sites among the pūkiawe and grass. Water is from a faucet on the trail near the cabin. Boil, filter, or chemically treat the water. There is one pit toilet in the campground and several more down by the cabin.

If you arrive at Hōlua early, explore a nearby lava tube. See tomorrow's narrative for directions. In the evening, watch the clouds retreating down Koʻolau Gap. Look at the sun's last rays hitting Hanakauhi peak across the gap. Feel the temperature plummet because of the clear skies and high elevation.

Route Description:

Retrace your steps along the Halemauʻu Trail.

Reach the signed junction near ʻŌʻilipuʻu (map point H). Turn right to Hōlua Cabin.

Ascend gradually through a grassy area with scattered pūkiawe and 'a'ali'i.

The grass narrows to a strip between two barren 'a'ā flows. The flow on the right issued from Kalua Awa vent on the crater wall. The trail follows or parallels several rocky gullies.

The grassy strip widens. On the right is a broad gully.

Bear left and climb a small *pali* (map point K).

On the left is a vegetated cinder cone known as Honokahua. The short climb to its top is well worth the effort.

Cross a short, flat, grassy section with an 'a'ā flow on the left.

Reach an obscure junction. Continue straight on the main trail. The unmaintained trail to the right and back skirts the crater wall.

On the right pass Mauna Hina (gray mountain), a steep cone covered with grass.

Cross several fingers of 'a'ā lava from a vent near Mauna Hina.

Pass close to Nāmanaokeakua (the powers of the god), an old vegetated cone on the left.

Reach a signed junction (map point L). Keep right for Hōlua Cabin. (The trail to the left leads to Kapalaoa Cabin.)

The vegetation thins. Underfoot are dark sand and cinders.

Part way up the ridge on the right are a series of huge rock dikes. They have eroded to look like the dorsal fins on a fish.

On the left pass Pu'u Nole (weak hill), a brown-black cone dotted with silverswords.

Reach a signed junction (map point M). Continue straight on the Halemau'u Trail. (The trail to the left leads to Kapalaoa Cabin.)

Ascend gradually around the right side of Pu'u Naue (earthquake hill) cone. It is colored red and grey and is also dotted with silverswords.

Almost immediately reach an obscure junction. Continue straight on the main trail. (The unmaintained trail to the right leads down Ko'olau Gap to the Waikau Cabin site.)

Descend briefly to reach the Bottomless Pit and still another junction. Continue straight, to Hōlua Cabin. (The trail to the left leads across the crater to Sliding Sands Trail.)

Go around the base of Halāli'i cone. At its back side are views down Ko'olau (windward) Gap and across the crater to Kalahaku (proclaim the lord) and Leleiwi (bone altar) Pali.

Reach a signed junction (map point N). Bear right to Hōlua Cabin. (The left fork leads to Sliding Sands Trail.)

Descend briefly and cross a basin covered with black sand, cinders, and lava rock.

Climb out of the basin on red cinders.

Reach a signed junction (map point O). Turn right on the Silversword Loop. (The main trail continues straight, to Hōlua Cabin.)

Wind through red-brown cinders dotted with silverswords.

Reach a signed junction with the main trail and turn right on it.

Enter an old 'a'ā flow partially covered with vegetation. In the distance you can see Hōlua Cabin, nestled against the crater wall.

Descend briefly on a rough trail.

Reach a signed junction in front of Hōlua Cabin (map point P). Continue straight to the cabin. (The trail to the right is the route out tomorrow.)

At the front lawn of the cabin turn left past the water faucet.

Climb briefly, but steeply, to Hōlua (sled) campground (elev. 6,960 ft).

DAY THREE—Hōlua to Haleakalā Crater Road

Length: 3.9 mi

Elev. Gain/Loss: 1,400/400 ft

Today you climb out of the crater. At least the route is short and has switchbacks on the steep ascent to the crater rim. Take your time, stop and admire the views, and you'll be on top before you know it.

Start early if you want to be sure of a clear view of the crater and Ko'olau Gap on the climb out. During the day, clouds often advance rapidly up the gap and can obscure the view from the switchbacks by mid-morning. Also, start reasonably early if you have only one car and it's parked at the Sliding Sands trailhead. That way you have more time to catch a ride back to your car.

If time and views are not a major consideration, explore the lava tube near the campground before leaving. To get there, follow these directions:

From the cabin, walk back along the Halemau'u Trail toward Palikū.

On the left pass a pit, which is actually part of a collapsed lava tube.

Just past the pit, turn right on a rough, makeshift trail. It may or may not be marked with small *ahu* (cairns).

Cross a brief stretch of *pāhoehoe* lava and then resume climbing on 'a'ā.

Reach a collapsed area that is the entrance to the lava tube.

Descend into the tube by means of a ladder.

At the bottom of the ladder walk straight ahead. (The tube also extends to the left behind you.)

Go around to the right of a boulder.

Climb steadily.

At the first fork keep left and down.
See a tiny shaft of light in the distance.
At the second fork keep left and climb.
Exit through the second opening in the ceiling.
On the right pick up an obscure trail that leads back to the campground.
The middle section of the tube is absolutely pitch black. Bring a good flashlight and extra batteries. The lava inside the tube is often sharp and brittle. Watch your head and hands. Wear a hat and gloves, if you have them.

Lava tubes are usually formed in *pāhoehoe* flows that are confined, such as in a gully. The top and edges of the flow cool and crust over. The lava inside continues to flow through the resulting tunnel. Eventually, the flow diminishes and stops, leaving a tube.

Route Description:

Walk back to the junction in front of the cabin (map point P). Turn left on the Halemau'u Trail. (The trail also continues straight, which is the way you came in yesterday.)

Descend Ko'olau Gap, gradually at first and then more steeply through ridges of jumbled up 'a'ā lava.

Work left toward the crater wall as the angle of descent eases.

Cross a meadow covered with evening primrose.

By a wooden gate and a hitching post, reach the base of the cliff and an obscure junction (map point Q). Go through the gate, closing it behind you. (The unmaintained trail to the right leads across Ko'olau Gap to the Waikau Cabin site.)

Begin climbing the crater wall on seven short switchbacks. The views back into the crater are spectacular.

Switchbacks eight through 12 are much longer and repeatedly cross a prominent side ridge in the cliff. You can now see down Ko'olau Gap as well as back into the crater.

After the twelfth switchback, follow the side ridge straight up (map point R).

Resume switchbacking as the slope steepens. The switchbacks are short and roughly parallel a fence on the right.

After the twentieth and last switchback (yes!), reach a metal gate at the crater rim. Go through the gate, closing it behind you.

Reach a junction (map point S). Keep left on the main trail. (The supply trail to the right leads down to Hosmer Grove campground.)

Ascend gradually along the slopes of Haleakalā below the crater rim. The trail is rough and eroded in spots.

Reach Halemau'u trailhead and parking lot (elev. 7,990 ft) (map point T). If your car is parked at Sliding Sands trailhead, hitchhike back up to it.

Options:

There are several variations of this trip. You can, of course, do the loop in reverse, stopping at Hōlua first and then Palikū. However, that makes for a long, hard third day up the Sliding Sands Trail. It is well named; for every two feet up you slide back one.

Groups with limited time can make a two-day trip. Descend to Palikū on the first day and climb out of the crater past Hōlua on the second. It's a pity, though, to miss camping at Hōlua, which is so very different from Palikū.

Parties with extra time can spend a layover day at Palikū or Hōlua. Both areas have some superb side trips. From Palikū you can take the Lau'ulu Trail to the crater rim and a view of the back of remote Kīpahulu Valley. The trail starts from the water faucet, skirts the campground, and begins climbing the ridge behind the cabin. Another shorter route to the rim is the steep Notch Trail. It starts in the pasture beyond the ranger cabin. From Hōlua you can take the trail across Ko'olau Gap to the Waikau Cabin site. The start of that trail is described in the Day Three narrative.

All of the side trips just mentioned use unmaintained trails, which are sometimes rough, narrow, and obscure. The Park Service neither encourages nor discourages their use. Try them only if you are an experienced hiker with good route-finding skills.

The last and perhaps best option is to continue from Palikū down Kaupō Gap to Kaupō town on the south coast of the island. The hike is a foot-pounding, knee-jarring descent of about 6,000 feet in 6.8 miles. The trail is maintained but is rough and rocky in spots. The main problem with this option is the complicated 100-mile shuttle necessary to leave a car at Kaupō. If possible, arrange to have someone pick you up at the trailhead. Otherwise, it's a long hitchhike back to the National Park.

O‘AHU

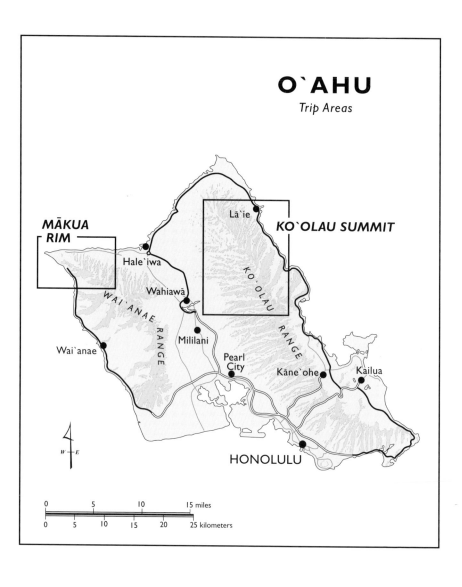

9. Ko'olau Summit

Type:	Mountain
Length:	3 days, 19.5 mi
Elev. Gain/Loss:	2,900/1,700 ft
Difficulty:	High
Location:	Ko'olau Range, O'ahu: Kahuku, Kawailoa and 'Ewa Forest Reserves
Topo Map:	Kahuku, Hau'ula

Highlights

This trip follows the wild, remote crest of the Ko'olau Range from Lā'ie to Wahiawā. Along the way are windy lookouts, 2,000-foot cliffs and an incredible variety of native rain forest plants. You may also encounter O'ahu's rainiest weather, deepest mud holes, and biggest pigs.

Planning

For the Lā'ie Trail on the first day, obtain a hiking permit from Hawaii Reserves, Inc., 55–510 Kamehameha Hwy, Lā'ie, HI 96762; phone (808) 293–9201. For the Schofield-Waikāne Trail on the last day, obtain written permission from the Directorate of Public Works, U.S. Army Garrison, Hawaii, Schofield Barracks, HI 96857. Request the permits for the two trails well in advance.

Early summer (May–July) is the best time of year to take this trip. The days are warm and long then, and the campsites usually have water. The trail is driest in late summer (August–October). If you plan to go then, bring extra water as the campsites may not have any.

The driving instructions start from downtown Honolulu. Arrange to be dropped off in Lā'ie and picked up in Wahiawā. Do not leave your car unattended for three days at either trailhead. The Honolulu Bus does serve both trailheads, but the drivers frequently won't let you board with a large pack and muddy boots.

Bring an internal frame pack and keep it streamlined. The route is far too rough and overgrown for an external frame pack. Also, take a tent as there is no shelter at Kawailoa, and the Poamoho Cabin is falling apart. Bring a light sleeping bag or liner as the nights can be chilly, even in summer. Pack all your dry gear in plastic bags.

Coleman fuel (white gas) is widely available in Honolulu. Check the nearest Longs Drug Store, 7-Eleven, or supermarket. Finally, prepare yourself mentally for the difficulties to be encountered. The weather is usually cloudy, wet, and often cool. The trail is rough, muddy, overgrown, and obscure, but rarely all at the same time. Expect the worst, and you may be pleasantly surprised. View the trip as a grand adventure, and you won't be disappointed.

Trailhead Directions—Lā'ie Trail

Distance: (downtown Honolulu to Lā'ie trailhead)—32 mi

Driving Time: one hr

At Punchbowl St. get on the Lunalilo Fwy (H-1) heading 'Ewa (west). Take Likelike Hwy (exit 20A, Rte 63 north) up Kalihi Valley through the Wilson Tunnel.

Turn left on Kahekili Hwy (Rte 83 west). That junction is the first major one after the tunnel and is marked Kahalu'u-Lā'ie.

Kahekili becomes Kamehameha Hwy (still Rte 83), which continues up the windward coast.

Drive through the villages of Ka'a'awa, Punalu'u, and Hau'ula to Lā'ie.

Pass the Polynesian Cultural Center and Lā'ie Shopping Center on the left.

Turn left on Naniloa Loop. That's the fourth left after the entrance road to the Mormon Temple. The loop has a grass median strip.

Enter a small traffic circle and exit at the second right on Po'ohaili St. Pull over on the grass to the left by a baseball field (map point A). Drop off people going on the trip. Do not leave your car at the trailhead.

Trailhead Directions—Schofield-Waikāne Trail

Distance: (downtown Honolulu to Schofield-Waikāne trailhead)—25 mi

Driving Time: 45 min

At Punchbowl St. get on the Lunalilo Fwy (H-1) heading 'Ewa (west). Near Middle St. keep left on Rte 78 west (exit 19B, Moanalua Rd.) to 'Aiea.

By Aloha Stadium bear right to rejoin H-1 to Pearl City. Take the H-2 Fwy (exit 8A) toward Wahiawā.

Get off H-2 at Wahiawā (exit 8, Rte 80 north).

At the end of the off ramp merge into Kamehameha Hwy.

Cross Wilson Bridge and enter Wahiawā town.
Just past Wendy's turn right on California Ave.
The road narrows to two lanes.
Pass Leilehua High School on the right.
The road jogs right and then left.
Drive to the end of California Ave. near two large, green water tanks (map point S).
Park there and wait for the people on the trip to come out.

DAY ONE—Lā'ie to Kawailoa

Length: 6.5 mi

Elev. Gain: 2,300 ft

The route today ascends to the top of the Ko'olau Range. The climbing is not steep, but it is steady. Start reasonably early because the first three miles of the hike are on a hot dirt road. The Lā'ie Trail is clear and well graded to the junction with the side trail to the pool. Beyond that junction the main trail becomes increasingly rough, muddy, and overgrown. It's a good preview of what the Ko'olau Summit Trail is like.

The Summit Trail is a contour or side hill trail. That means it was built into the side of the summit ridge, not along its top. Sometimes the trail is on the windward (left) side and sometimes on the leeward (right) side. When on the windward side, the Summit Trail is usually clear, although still rough and muddy. When on the leeward side, the trail is rough, muddy, and overgrown. Learn to appreciate the windward sections and grit your teeth while plowing through the leeward ones.

Today's hike includes only a short ½-mile stretch on the Summit Trail to the Kawailoa Ridge Trail junction, the first campsite. Pitch your tent on the leeward side of the helipad in a small grassy area next to some metal landing mats. If you and your tent don't mind the heavy trade winds, camp on top of the helipad with its 360 degree view.

From the helipad you can see Lā'ie and Hau'ula towns far below to windward. On the leeward side is the north shore from Hale'iwa town to Ka'ena Point. In the distance is the Wai'anae Range. The gap in the mountains is Kolekole Pass. The two peaks to the right of the pass are Kalena and flat-topped Mt. Ka'ala, the highest on O'ahu at 4,025 ft. Directly below the helipad are the headwaters of Kawainui and Kamananui Streams, separated by the Kawailoa Ridge Trail. All around is the convoluted topography of the northern Ko'olau Range.

The water source is the sluggish stream you crossed just before reaching the base of the helipad. Boil, filter, or chemically treat the water.

If you still have some energy and time after setting up camp, explore down the Kawailoa Ridge Trail. After dinner, watch the sunset near Ka'ena Pt.

Route Description:

Continue along Po'ohaili St. on foot.

After passing the last house, go through a yellow gate.

Just past some guard rails the road becomes dirt.

Reach a fork. Keep left, past a utility pole.

Shortly afterward the road forks again. This time keep right, following the line of utility poles.

Pass several aquaculture ponds and a pump shack on the right.

Reach a junction. Take the right fork across a small concrete bridge.

At the next junction turn left uphill through a turquoise gate (map point B).

At the next fork bear left, again uphill. (The right fork leads to an open dirt area.)

Another dirt road comes in on the left. Continue straight past some ironwoods.

At the next fork keep right, hugging the ridge.

Pass a barbed wire fence extending left and right.

Curve right and then left on the road, now deeply rutted.

Reach another junction. Take the right, more eroded fork.

At an open flat area keep right uphill on a very eroded section of the road.

The road narrows to a trail and is flanked by uluhe ferns and strawberry guavas.

Reach a grove of Norfolk Island pines (map point C). The Lā'ie Trail starts in the grove along the ridge line.

Descend briefly through the last of the pines.

Climb gradually along the left side of the ridge through a long stretch of strawberry guavas.

Right after the guavas switch to uluhe ferns, reach a junction (map point D). Keep left toward the summit. (To the right and up a low embankment is a short but steep trail that leads down to a small pool and two waterfalls along Kahawainui Stream.)

Ascend gradually in and out of the small side gulches.

Pass an open stretch with a steep cliff on the right and sharp drop-off on the left.

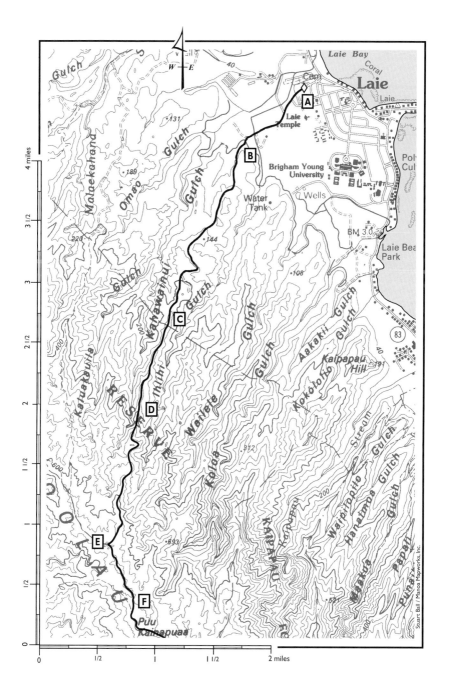

Bear left and down into a gully to cross a large landslide blocking the original trail.

After climbing out of the gully, turn left and continue the gradual ascent along the side of the ridge.

Reach the ridge line and cross over to the right side of the ridge.

The gulch on the right narrows.

Work up the side of the gulch toward its end at the summit ridge.

Just before the top the trail forks. Take the left fork.

Shortly afterward reach the junction with the Koʻolau Summit Trail (map point E). Turn left on it. (To the right the Summit Trail leads to Pūpūkea Rd.)

Before starting for the Kawailoa Ridge Trail junction, drop your pack and climb the low mound on the right to reach the actual Koʻolau summit (elev. 2,240 ft). If the weather is clear, you can see Kahuku and Lāʻie towns to windward. The Wahiawā plain and the Waiʻanae Range are to leeward.

Go around a small knob on its leeward (right) side.

Switch to the windward (left) side of the ridge.

Contour below a series of low hills on the summit ridge.

Pass several open grassy areas and a stand of Australian tea shrubs.

Switch to the leeward (right) side of the ridge. You can see the Kawailoa Ridge Trail on the side ridge to the right.

A flat-topped mound occasionally used as a helipad comes into view on the right. Its windward side has a collapsed wooden platform.

Descend gradually and work right, through a grove of Australian tea shrubs in a marshy area.

Cross a sluggish stream on metal landing mats.

Near the base of the helipad reach the junction with the Kawailoa Ridge Trail (map point F). Turn right on it and go around the helipad.

Camp on the leeward side of the helipad or on top.

DAY TWO—Kawailoa to Poamoho

Length: 5.9 mi

Elev. Gain/Loss: 600/300 ft

Today is a long, tough day, perhaps the roughest in this book. Start early because travel on the Summit Trail is pathetically slow, ½ to one mile per hour. You get stuck in mud holes and tangled in vegetation as well as losing the trail a few times.

The Summit Trail continues the pattern of switching from the windward to the leeward side and back again. When the trail needs to gain or lose elevation quickly, it uses switchbacks. The trail never goes up or down a ridge line or valley bottom. If you find yourself on a narrow path heading down a side ridge or into a gulch, you are following a pig trail, not the Summit Trail. Turn around and backtrack to the main route before you get lost.

Feral pigs make up most of the traffic on the Summit Trail. They usually detect you first and move off the trail. Pigs are not aggressive unless cornered so give them plenty of room to retreat if you do encounter them on the trail. As you can see, their rooting has severely damaged the native plants along parts of the trail, thus allowing introduced species to gain a foothold.

The Summit Trail passes through the native rain forest of O'ahu. Dominant are 'ōhi'a trees and uluhe fern in the open areas. 'Ōhi'a generally has small dark green leaves and clusters of delicate red flowers. Uluhe is the yellow-green scratchy fern, which is gradually ripping up your pants.

Two other common trees are the loulu palm and lapalapa. You can see both of them during the first mile today and periodically thereafter. Lapalapa has yellow-green rounded leaves that flutter in the slightest breeze. The name derives from the sound the leaves make in the wind.

Loulu is the only palm native to Hawai'i. Along the summit it occurs individually or in clumps. The leaves are fan shaped and were used by the Hawaiians as umbrellas and house thatch.

The Cline memorial at Poamoho lists the mileage to each junction on the Summit Trail. Geraldine Cline was a beloved member of the Hawaiian Trail and Mountain Club on O'ahu. She died tragically in an automobile accident.

The Poamoho campsite is a lovely spot nestled in a gulch on the leeward side of the summit ridge. The site is still windy, but much less so than the summit near the Cline memorial. Water is usually available from the stream in front of the camp or from a drip upstream in the hillside on the right. As always, boil, filter, or chemically treat the water.

If you actually have time and energy to spare after setting up camp, explore down the Poamoho Trail. After dinner, walk back up to the Summit lookout and watch night fall. The view there is one of the best on O'ahu. Below lie Punalu'u and Kahana Valleys. The sharp peak to the right is Pu'u 'Ōhulehule. In front of it and partially hidden is Ka'a'awa Valley.

Route Description:

Climb to the top of the helipad.

While facing windward, turn right and proceed along the ridge on a narrow trail.

Shortly afterward, look for the Summit Trail below on the left. It comes out of the Australian tea grove, up a gully, and then turns sharp left.

Descend the open slope on the left to the Summit Trail and turn right on it.

Contour on the windward (left) side of the summit ridge below two hills, known as Pu'u Ka'inapua'a (pig procession hill).

Pass several stands of loulu palm and lapalapa with its light green fluttering leaves. Feral pigs have ripped up some of the native vegetation along the trail in this area.

Switch to the leeward (right) side of the ridge briefly and then switch back to windward.

The trail crosses over to the leeward side.

Climb steeply to the left to bypass a blocked trail section.

Shortly afterward, switch to the windward side for a long stretch. The trail is very muddy with deep holes.

The trail crosses over to the leeward side for a short while. There are views down Kawainui Stream.

Switch to the windward side of the summit ridge.

Walk through a flat open area with views to windward. The back of Koloa Gulch is on the left.

Pass the stacked remains of the Kahuku Cabin on the left (map point G).

Keep left and descend briefly through a narrow defile.

Reach an overlook of spectacular Kaipapa'u Gulch (map point H).

The trail is cut into the steep cliff at the back of the gulch.

Negotiate a deep gut in the trail.

Switch to the leeward side to go around a large hump in the ridge.

Pass a huge rock in the middle of the trail. Climb steadily.

The trail levels out in a grassy area with views of the windward side.

Continue on the leeward side for a long stretch.

The windward coast comes into view again.

Switch to the windward side and traverse a relatively level section.

The trail crosses over to the leeward side and then back to windward. Climb gradually.

Switch to the leeward side for a long section.

Switch to the windward side and then back to leeward.

Along the Nā Pali Coast. Kalalau trip. (Photo by Deborah Uchida)

Sunset at Kalalau Beach. Kalalau trip. (Photo by Deborah Uchida)

'Āhinahina, the Haleakalā silversword. Haleakalā trip. (Photo by Deborah Uchida)

Kawaikōī Stream. Mōhihi-Koaiʻe trip. (Photo by Deborah Uchida)

Mist settling over Koaiʻe Stream. Mōhihi-Koaiʻe trip. (Photo by Deborah Uchida)

Clouds riding up Koʻolau Gap. Haleakalā trip. (Photo by Deborah Uchida)

Across the crater toward Palikū. Haleakalā trip. (Photo by Deborah Uchida)

Mākua Valley. Mākua Rim trip. (Photo by Deborah Uchida)

Puʻu ʻŌʻō erupting at dusk. Nāpau Crater trip. (Photo by Jason Sunada)

Hiking down the Sliding Sands Trail. Haleakalā trip. (Photo by Deborah Uchida)

Skirting mudholes along
the Summit Trail.
Ko'olau Summit trip.
(Photo by Deborah
Uchida)

Lava tube, tree molds,
and Pu'u 'Ō'ō cone.
Nāpau Crater trip.
(Photo by Jason Sunada)

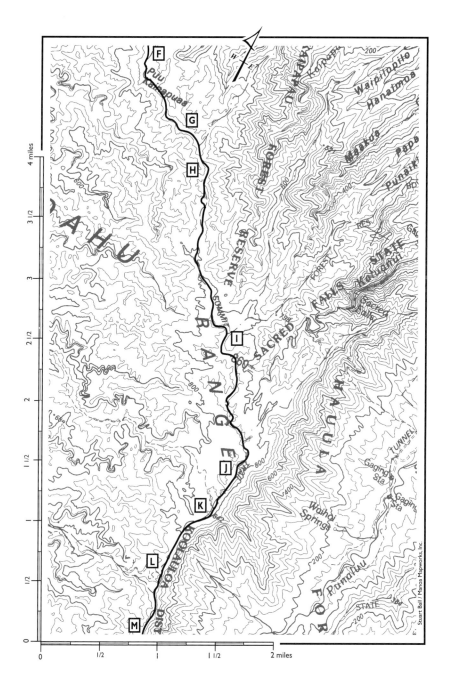

The trail crosses over to the windward side of the summit ridge and climbs steadily.

On top of the ridge reach a junction marked by a metal stake (map point I). Continue straight on the Summit Trail. (To the left the Castle Trail leads down to Punalu'u Valley.)

Switch to the leeward side and then back to windward.

Go around a large bowl-shaped area. Down and to the left is a small solar-powered weather station.

Pass some metal landing mats on the left.

The trail crosses over to the leeward side and then back to windward.

Traverse an open scenic section at the back of Kaluanui Stream. The low hills there are the highest point on the trip at just over 2,800 feet.

Switch to the leeward side of the summit ridge.

Cross a small grassy area and swing left. To leeward you can see the Wai'anae Range and Wahiawā town.

Switch to the windward side and cross another grassy spot.

Cross over to the leeward side.

Emerge onto a windswept grassy area with a top of a waterfall notch on the left. Water is sometimes available in the notch

Climb gradually, continuing on the leeward side.

Reach an awesome overlook (map point J). Punalu'u Valley is 2,000 feet below. Behind it is Kahana Valley with Pu'u 'Ōhulehule on the right.

Cross a windy grassy area covered with landing mats.

As the trail turns sharp left, reach a junction (map point K). Keep left on the Summit Trail. (To the right the Pe'ahināi'a Trail leads down to Hale'iwa).

The trail remains on the leeward side but passes a series of tantalizing view points of the windward valleys. You can see the Summit Trail in the distance as it goes below Pu'u Pauao.

Switch briefly to the windward side and descend steeply.

Cross over to the leeward side again.

Finally, switch to the windward side of the summit ridge (yea!). The narrow trail is cut into the near vertical cliff. Watch your footing. Don't look at the view and walk at the same time. The views really open up. Behind Kahana Valley are Ka'a'awa, Hakipu'u, and Waikāne Valleys. Beyond is Kāne'ohe Bay and the windward coast to Makapu'u Point.

Climb up and over a small landslide.

Switch to the leeward side and descend briefly.

Reach a junction marked by the stone Cline memorial (map point L). Turn right, down the Poamoho Trail, to reach the campsite. (To the left is a windy overlook. Straight ahead the Summit Trail continues to Poamoho Cabin.)

On the Poamoho Trail cross a windy grassy area.

Descend gradually to a small stream and cross it to the right.

Almost immediately reach a flat grassy area on the left which is the campsite.

DAY THREE—Poamoho to Wahiawā

Length: 8.1 mi

Elev. Loss: 1,400 ft

The route today is mostly downhill, but it's still a long haul over rough, overgrown trails. Don't expect to get out much before late afternoon.

In the morning continue along the Ko'olau Summit Trail past the Poamoho Cabin and beneath massive Pu'u Pauao. The cabin is not a pleasant place to spend the night as it is gradually falling apart. There is still water in the tank nearby.

Much of the trail lies on the windward side so the views are panoramic. From the Schofield-Waikāne junction you can see four undeveloped valleys below. From left to right they are Kahana, Ka'a'awa, Hakipu'u, and Waikāne. Pu'u 'Ōhulehule is now directly *makai* (seaward). Look along the summit ridge and trace the trail as it climbs in back of Pu'u Ka'aumakua (family deity hill) on the way to Kīpapa. Descending along the side ridge below Pu'u Ka'aumakua is the Waikāne Trail.

Take one last look at the view and then leave the summit on the Schofield-Waikāne Trail. It's in slightly better condition than the Summit Trail. The upper section is usually overgrown with uluhe. The trail opens up some as you approach the U.S. Army road.

Route Description:
Walk back up the Poamoho Trail.

At the Cline memorial turn right on the Ko'olau Summit Trail.

Initially, contour on the leeward (right) side of the ridge.

Switch to the windward (left) side and go around several low hills.

The trail crosses over to the leeward side.

Reach the Poamoho Cabin (map point M).

Switch to the windward side and then back to leeward.

Cross over to the windward side for a long scenic stretch below Pu'u Pauao (map point N).

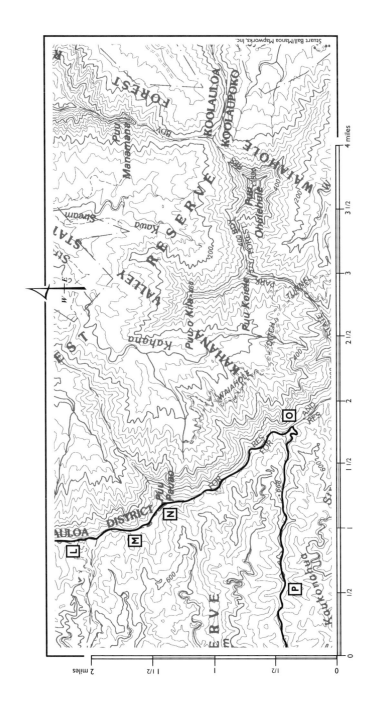

Stuart Ball/Manoa Mapworks, Inc.

Contour below a large hump in the summit ridge.

Shortly afterward, as the trail goes along the top of the ridge, reach a junction (map point O). Turn right, down the Schofield-Waikāne Trail. (The Summit Trail continues straight and leads to the Waikāne and Kīpapa Ridge Trails.)

On the left pass a small open area with good views of the Wai'anae Range.

Step on some metal roofing, all that's left of an old shelter.

Descend steadily along the crest of the side ridge. The trail contours to the right once and to the left twice to skirt humps in the ridge.

Cross a relatively level section on top of the ridge (map point P).

Descend gradually on the left side of the ridge for a long stretch. Occasionally, the trail shifts briefly to the actual ridge line or to its right side.

Reach a junction. Keep left on the main ridge. (The trail to the right leads down to the north fork of Kaukonahua Stream.)

Switch to the right side of the ridge.

Jump over a deep but narrow cut in the ridge.

Ascend briefly on a switchback.

Reach the end of the Schofield-Waikāne Trail at a junction with a dirt road (map point Q). Turn right on it.

Descend steadily along the ridge top. The road switches back several times on the steeper sections.

As the ridge flattens out, reach a junction with another dirt road (map point R). Keep right, on the main road.

Pass a series of Army training areas in the East Range.

Before passing a cluster of buildings on the left, look for two large green water tanks on the right.

Leave the road and angle right, toward the tanks through a eucalyptus forest.

Reach the fence surrounding the tanks and bear right along it.

Emerge into civilization at the end of California Ave. in Wahiawā (map point S).

Options:

There are potentially lots of variations on this trip, but most of them can get you into trouble very quickly. You can do the trip in reverse; however, the first two days become very hard and the last day, quite easy. The route as described spreads the difficulty more evenly over the three days. Also, it allows you to gracefully bail out down the Lā'ie Trail if you don't like what you're getting into.

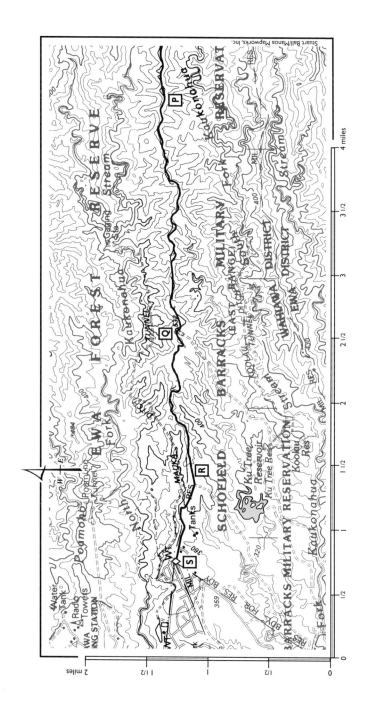

Stuart Ball/Manoa Mapworks, Inc.

The route of this trip intersects with four other recognized trails: Kawailoa, Castle, Pe'ahināi'a, and Poamoho. None of them makes a good entrance or exit because they are all closed to the public or heavily overgrown or both.

The Ko'olau Summit Trail continues past the Schofield-Waikāne Trail junction to the Waikāne and Kīpapa Ridge Trails. Both are closed to the public and heavily overgrown. After the Waikāne junction, the Summit Trail stays on the leeward side of the ridge and is choked with *Clidemia hirta* shrubs and uluhe fern.

In the other direction, the Summit Trail continues past the Lā'ie Trail junction all the way to Pūpūkea Rd. That section is severely overgrown with guava and uluhe fern. You can, however, get permission to do it from the U.S. Army.

10. Mākua Rim

Type:	Mountain
Length:	2–3 days, 13.5 mi round trip
Elev. Gain/Loss:	1,100/1,100 ft
Difficulty:	Low
Location:	Wai'anae Range, O'ahu: Kuaokalā Forest Reserve, Pahole Natural Area Reserve
Topo Map:	Ka'ena

Highlights

This trip follows the Wai'anae summit ridge along the cliffs of Keawa'ula and the rim of Mākua Valley. On the way you see remnants of native dry-land forest in the Pahole Natural Area Reserve. The secluded campsite, tucked below the valley rim, features one of the most breathtaking overlooks in the islands.

Planning

Get a hiking/camping permit from the State Forestry Division in downtown Honolulu. Their office is in the Kalanimoku Building, Room 325, 1151 Punchbowl St., across from the State Capitol; phone (808) 587–0166. Hours are 7:45 A.M.– 4:30 P.M., Monday to Friday. While there, pick up Forestry's excellent trail map of the Kuaokalā-Mokulē'ia area. The driving instructions below start from the Kalanimoku Building.

Take this trip in late winter (February–April). The weather is cooler then and the landscape, greener. You also miss bird, pig, and goat hunting season. If you must go in season, wear bright colored clothing.

Bring a tent as the picnic shelter does not provide sufficient protection from wind or rain. The shelter is also wide open to cockroaches and other night crawlers. Take a light sleeping bag or liner as the nights can be chilly, especially in winter. The campsite has a few lazy mosquitoes so bring repellant if you wish.

If you have recently hiked in the Ko'olau Range on O'ahu, clean the sides and soles of your boots before taking this trip. Hikers spread the seeds of *Clidemia hirta*, an aggressive, introduced shrub, that clogs many of the Ko'olau trails. The Pahole Natural Area Reserve is still relatively free of this pest. Let's keep it that way.

Coleman fuel (white gas) is widely available in Honolulu. Check the nearest 7-Eleven, Longs Drug Store, or supermarket.

Trailhead Directions

Distance: (Downtown Honolulu to Kuaokalā trailhead)—43 mi

Driving Time: 1 hr

At Punchbowl St. get on the Lunalilo Fwy (H-1) heading 'Ewa (west). Near Middle St. keep left on Rte 78 west (exit 19B-Moanalua Rd.) to 'Aiea.

By Aloha Stadium bear right to rejoin H-1 to Pearl City and on toward Wai'anae.

As the freeway ends near Campbell Industrial Park, continue along the leeward (west) coast on Farrington Hwy (Rte 93).

Pass the Kahe Pt. power plant on the right.

Drive through Nānākuli, Mā'ili, and Wai'anae towns.

The road narrows to two lanes.

Drive through Mākaha and pass Kea'au Beach Park on the left.

On the right pass 'Ōhikilolo Mākua Ranch and then Mākua Military Reservation with its observation post.

Reach the end of the paved highway at Keawa'ula (Yokohama) Bay.

Turn right on the access road to the Ka'ena Pt. Satellite Tracking Sta.

Show your permit and an ID at the guard station and get a visitor pass.

Switchback up Kuaokalā Ridge.

At its top turn right at the T intersection on Road B.

Curve left by the main administration building.

Pass a paved one-lane road on the right through some ironwood trees.

After a short descent look for a dirt lot on the right. It's just after another paved one-lane road comes in on the right.

Park in the lot (elev. 1,300 ft) (map point A).

DAY ONE—Ka'ena Pt. Satellite Tracking Station to Pahole Natural Area Reserve

Length: 6.6 mi

Elev. Gain: 1,100 ft

The first day's route travels on two of the most scenic trails on the island. The Kuaokalā (back of the sun) Trail hugs the cliffs above

Keawa'ula (red harbor) and leads to the first overlook of Mākua Valley. The Mākua Rim Trail follows the edge of that valley through the Pahole Natural Area Reserve to the campsite.

Both trails have a mixture of graded sections with switchbacks and non-graded sections with straight ups and downs. Start reasonably early because there is plenty to see along the route and near the campsite.

Several cautions are in order for today. Watch out for the occasional four-wheel-drive vehicle on the Kuaokalā Access Rd. Also, don't descend into Mākua Valley as it is a military range used for live fire exercises. Finally, tread lightly through the Pahole Reserve without picking or otherwise damaging the vegetation.

The Pahole Natural Area Reserve was established to preserve remnants of native dryland forest. The predominant trees along the trail are 'ōhi'a and koa. You can recognize 'ōhi'a by its clusters of delicate red flowers and koa by its sickle-shaped leaves. Less frequently seen are 'akoko and 'iliahi (sandalwood). Common shrubs along the trail are pūkiawe and 'a'ali'i. Pūkiawe has narrow, rigid leaves, and small white, pink, or red fruits. 'A'ali'i has narrow shiny green leaves and red seed capsules. You can also see the native herb, ko'oko'olau. It has bright yellow flowers with five petals.

You may run into feral pigs on or near the trail. They are not aggressive unless cornered and will usually run upon sighting you. Their rooting severely damages the native forest, thus allowing introduced species to take over. The cackling bird you will hear, but probably not see, is Erckel's francolin. It is a brown game bird originally from Africa.

The rim lookout (map point I) is an awesome spot. One thousand feet below lies the green expanse of Mākua Valley leading to the ocean. In back are the dark sheer walls of 'Ōhikilolo Ridge. Spend some time watching the interplay of sun and clouds on ocean, ridge, and valley. Who says O'ahu isn't as beautiful as the Neighbor Islands?

Camp in the flat area across Mokulē'ia Trail from the picnic shelter. If it's raining, the shelter makes a good cooking area.

To get to the water source from the shelter, turn right on the Mokulē'ia Trail. Descend gradually, switchbacking twice. Enter a deep gulch where the trail crosses a small stream. Walk upstream and fill your water bag or bottle. Boil, filter, or chemically treat the water.

In the evening walk to the valley overlook to watch the sun set and the stars come out. To get there turn left on the rim trail and climb steeply, but briefly.

Route Description:

From the lot walk across the side road and pick up the Kuaokalā Trail. The trailhead is marked by a Smokey the Bear sign.

Contour around a hill topped by ironwood trees.

Gain the ridge line (map point B) and bear left along it.

Stroll through ironwoods and introduced pines. There are good views of the leeward coast.

Contour on the right side of the ridge below its top.

Descend briefly into a shallow, wooded ravine. Climb alongside it.

At the end of the ravine turn left along the edge of the ridge (map point C).

Cross an eroded area and bear right, following the main ridge.

Traverse a narrow bare section.

Climb briefly to a copse of ironwood trees.

Ascend a small hill to an overlook of Mākua Valley (map point D).

Bear left along the rim of the valley.

Cross an open grassy stretch.

Pass another overlook with rock slabs.

Descend briefly and then climb steeply through eucalyptus to reach the end of a dirt road (elev. 1,960 ft).

Walk down the road away from the rim.

Reach a junction with the Kuaokalā Access Rd. (map point E). Turn a sharp right on it. (To the left the road leads back to the tracking station and is the return route on the second day.) Watch for four-wheel-drive vehicles on the road.

Descend along the rim, curving left and then right.

Bear left away from the rim to go around a hump on the ridge.

Regain the rim briefly and then swing left again to bypass a large hill on the ridge.

Reach a junction (map point F). Keep right, on the main road back toward the rim. (The grassy road heading down the side ridge to the left is the old Peacock Flat Trail. Don't venture on it because the trail is closed to the public.)

An abandoned Nike missile site comes into view across the gulch on the left.

As the road turns a sharp left and down to go around the Nike site, turn right and up on an overgrown dirt road (map point G).

Climb steadily along the forested rim.

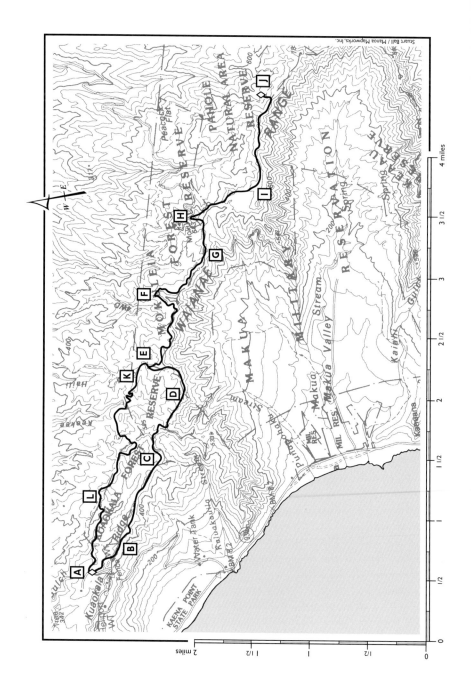

Break out into the open for a short level stretch. You can look down a gulch into Mākua Valley.

Resume steep climbing on the road. There are several short switch-backs.

Just past a metal stake the angle of ascent eases.

Pass a water tank on the left.

Almost immediately, reach an overlook with a bench mark (elev. 2,108 ft) (map point H). From there you can see the whole north shore of Oʻahu.

Near the bench mark, turn sharp right on the Mākua Rim Trail. (The road continues straight and then becomes a trail leading down to the Nike site.)

Descend briefly to a narrow saddle in the ridge. There are views of both the leeward coast and the north shore.

Contour right, around a bump in the ridge.

Enter Pahole Natural Area Reserve. Native dryland forest vegetation begins to predominate.

Bear left off the ridge line and ascend the side of a hill on 12 short switchbacks.

Climb steadily along the broad ridge. Keep to its left edge.

Keep right at a small eroded section.

As the ridge narrows, break out into the open for a short stretch.

Ascend gradually along the ridge, now wider. Again, keep to its left side.

Reach a breathtaking overlook along the Mākua rim (map point I). Across the valley are the imposing flanks of ʻŌhikilolo Ridge.

Turn left along the rim and descend gradually. Memorize that turn for the return trip.

Climb, steeply at times, over four humps, each one higher than the last.

Traverse a relatively level section.

Descend two short but steep stretches.

At the bottom of the second, pass two Norfolk Island pines on the left.

Climb and then descend steeply to a notch and a signed junction. Turn left and down off the ridge. (The Mākua Rim Trail continues straight and leads to the Mt. Kaʻala Rd.)

Descend to the Mokuleʻia campsite (elev. 2,180 ft) (map point J). On the left is a picnic shelter. The Mokuleʻia Trail runs through the campsite. To the right it goes to the water source. To the left the trail leads down to Peacock Flat and the Mokuleʻia Access Rd.

DAY TWO—Pahole Natural Area Reserve to Ka'ena Pt. Satellite Tracking Station

Length: 6.9 mi

Elev. Loss: 1,100 ft

If you have time in the morning, try one of the side trips mentioned under Options. On each, you can go as far as you want and then turn around.

The first part of the route today is a backtrack along the Mākua Rim Trail and the Kuaokalā Access Rd. If you are tired of road walking, turn left at map point E and return the way you came in, on the Kuaokalā Trail. Otherwise, continue on the access road.

The road offers some great views of the north shore from Hale'iwa town to Waimea Bay. In the distance to the west is the Ko'olau Range. Watch the fixed-wing gliders soaring above Dillingham Airfield. Sometimes, a plane will suddenly drop a load of colorful parachutists.

The route narrative refers to the main or through road and the old road. The main road is the well-graded and traveled road. The old road consists of rough, eroded sections that leave and then rejoin the main road. The route description follows the old sections where possible because they are shorter and have less vehicle traffic. You can, of course, take the main road all the way back.

Route Description:

Retrace your steps along the Mākua Rim Trail and the Kuaokalā Access Rd. to map point E.

Today, continue straight on the access road. (The road to the left leads to the Kuaokalā Trail and is the route you followed the first day.)

Reach the junction with the Keālia Trail (map point K). Keep left and down on the main road. (To the right, the Keālia Trail, which is a dirt road here, leads down to Dillingham Airfield on the Mokulē'ia side.)

At the next fork, turn sharp left on a section of the old road.

Descend steeply into Ke'eke'e Gulch.

At the bottom of the gulch rejoin the through road.

As the road splits again, keep left uphill on the through road.

The old road comes in on the right.

Descend and then bear left on a section of the old road.

Rejoin the through road.

At the next fork keep right on the through road.

The old road comes in on the left.
The road forks again by some gate posts (map point L). Bear left and down on a section of the old road.
Descend into Manini Gulch.
Rejoin the through road and parallel the stream bed.
Reach the end of a paved road by a water pump.
Take the road up out of the gulch.
Reach the dirt parking lot on the right (map point A).

Options:

There are two variations of this trip, neither as interesting as the route previously described. You can hike up the paved Mokulēʻia Access Rd. from Farrington Hwy. Turn left by Peacock Flat and pick up the Mokulēʻia Trail to the campsite.

For a harder trip, take the Keālia Trail which starts in back of Dillingham Air Field. Switchback up a *pali* (cliff) and join the Kuaokalā Access Rd. at map point K. Turn left on the road and follow the above narrative to the campsite.

From the campsite are two superb side trips. If you have the energy, try one late the first day or early the second. Better yet, spend an extra day at the campsite and try both.

The first side trip goes down the Mokulēʻia Trail past the water supply along a lovely forested ridge. Stop at the reserve boundary because the pasture land below is private property. Return uphill the way you came.

The other side trip continues along the Mākua Rim Trail toward Mt. Kaʻala. Ascend two significant humps in the ridge. After the second, descend very steeply and then climb a broad hill where ʻŌhikilolo Ridge comes in on the right. Return the same way. Along the route are spectacular views of the north shore and Mākua Valley.

APPENDIX: CLOSED TRIPS

The three trips briefly described below are among the best in the Islands. Unfortunately, they are all currently closed to the general public for one or both of these reasons.

1. The trip crosses private property, and the landowner will not grant permission under any circumstance.

2. The route is not maintained, and sections of it have become virtually impassable because of fallen trees, landslides, or washouts.

Kohala Ditch

Kohala Ditch is a rugged loop trip in the windward Kohala Mountains of the Big Island. The route initially traverses several massive ridges and deep canyons with fast flowing streams. The return portion is along the coast where black sand beaches alternate with steep sea cliffs. Much of the trail follows an abandoned ditch, once used to channel stream water to a sugar cane plantation near Hāwī.

Mōhihi-Waiʻalae

Mōhihi-Waiʻalae is a challenging loop trip through the Alakaʻi Swamp on the island of Kauaʻi. The first section is open and is fully described as Trip No. 7, Mōhihi-Koaiʻe. From Koaiʻe Camp, the closed route continues through the swamp and eventually turns down Kaluahāʻula Ridge into Waimea Canyon.

This trip might reopen when the Kauaʻi Division of Forestry finishes clearing damage from hurricane ʻIniki. Inquire at their office listed under Trip No. 7 for the current status.

Wailau

The Wailau trip traverses the island of Molokaʻi from south to north. From the leeward south coast the route gradually climbs to the summit ridge. The trail then plunges down the steep windward *pali* (cliff) into Wailau Valley. The trip ends at a remote black sand beach framed by vertical sea cliffs.

SUGGESTED REFERENCES

Ball, Stuart M. Jr. *The Hikers Guide to O'ahu*. Honolulu: University of Hawai'i Press, 1993.

Berger, Andrew J. *Hawaiian Birdlife*, 2d ed. Honolulu: University of Hawai'i Press, 1988.

Bier, James A. Map of Hawai'i, 5th ed. Honolulu: University of Hawai'i Press, 1993.

———. Map of Kaua'i, 4th ed. Honolulu: University of Hawai'i Press, 1991.

———. Map of Maui, 5th ed. Honolulu: University of Hawai'i Press, 1993.

———. Map of O'ahu, 5th ed. Honolulu: University of Hawai'i Press, 1996.

———. O'ahu Reference Maps, 3d ed. Champaign, Ill.

Bryan's Sectional Maps of O'ahu, 1994 ed. Honolulu: EMIC Graphics, 1993.

Carlquist, Sherman. *Hawaii, a Natural History*, 2d ed. Lawai, Hi.: Pacific Tropical Botanical Garden, 1980.

Chisholm, Craig. *Hawaiian Hiking Trails*. Lake Oswego, Or.: The Fernglen Press, 1989.

Department of Health. What is Leptospirosis? (pamphlet). Honolulu, 1992.

Department of Land and Natural Resources. Pahole Natural Area Reserve (pamphlet). 1994.

———. Recreation Map of Western Kauai. Honolulu.

———. Waimanu Natural Estuarine Research Reserve (pamphlet).

Hawaii Audubon Society. *Hawaii's Birds*. Honolulu, 1989.

Koke'e Trails (pamphlet).

Krauss, Beatrice H. *Plants in Hawaiian Culture*. Honolulu: University of Hawai'i Press, 1993.

Lamoureux, Charles H. *Trailside Plants of Hawaii's National Parks*. Hawaii Natural History Association and Hawaii Volcanoes National Park, 1976.

MacDonald, Gordon A., Agatin T. Abbott, and Frank L. Peterson. *Volcanoes in the Sea*, 2d ed. Honolulu: University of Hawai'i Press, 1990.

McMahon, Richard. *Camping Hawai'i*. Honolulu: University of Hawai'i Press, 1994.

Miller, Carey D., Katherine Bazore, and Mary Bartow. *Fruits of Hawaii*. Honolulu: University of Hawai'i Press, 1991.

National Park Service. Haleakala National Park (pamphlet).

———. Hawaii Volcanoes National Park (pamphlet).

Petersen, Lisa. *Mauna Loa Trail Guide*, 2d ed. Hawaii Natural History Association, 1992.

Pukui, Mary Kawena, and Samuel H. Elbert. *Hawaiian Dictionary*. Honolulu: University of Hawai'i Press, 1986.

Pukui, Mary Kawena, Samuel H. Elbert, and Esther T. Mookini. *Place Names of Hawaii.* Honolulu: University of Hawai'i Press, 1981.

Sohmer, S. H., and R. Gustafson. *Plants and Flowers of Hawai'i.* Honolulu: University of Hawai'i Press, 1987.

United States Geological Survey. Hawaii Volcanoes National Park and Vicinity (map). 1986.

University of Hawaii. *Atlas of Hawaii,* 2d ed. Honolulu: University of Hawai'i Press, 1983.

Valier, Kathy. *On the Nā Pali Coast.* Honolulu: University of Hawai'i Press, 1989.

Wagner, Warren L., Derral R. Herbst, and S. H. Sohmer. *Manual of the Flowering Plants of Hawai'i.* Honolulu: University of Hawai'i Press and Bishop Museum Press, 1990.

INDEX

References to maps are in **boldface**